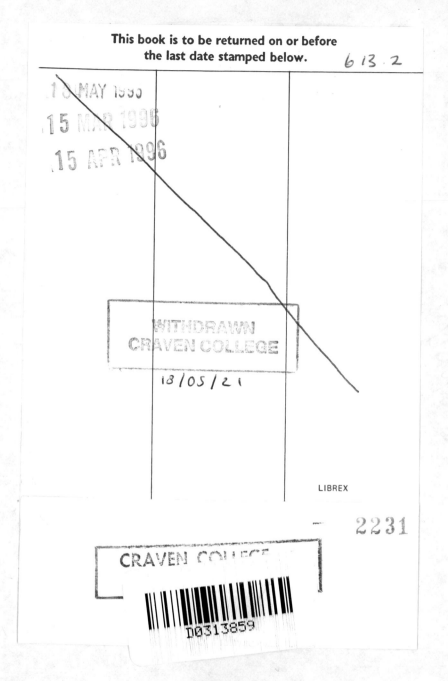

Healthy Eating
a guide for chefs and caterers

Rob Silverstone, BSc (Hons)

Foreword by Drew Smith, Consumers' Association

MACMILLAN

First published 1990

Published by
MACMILLAN EDUCATION LTD
Houndmills, Basingstoke, Hampshire RG21 2XS
and London
Companies and representatives
throughout the world

Printed in Hong Kong

British Library Cataloguing in Publication Data
Silverstone, Rob
Healthy eating: a guide to chefs and caterers
1. Health food
I. Title
641.3′02
ISBN 0–333–52260–5

To Grandma Fischmann, who inspired us all to greater things in the kitchen

Contents

Part II THE RECIPES

Acknowledgements

I am indebted to Dr Nick Light, Wendy Doyle, Dr James Jones, Denise Worsfold and John Valentine for invaluable professional advice. Thanks also to Joy and Dot for typing, Gareth for photography, and Betty for the illustration.

Note: nutritional advice for readers in the United States. The nutritional advice in this book is based upon dietary guidelines issued in the United Kingdom by the NACNE and COMA Committees. These guidelines are equally applicable in the United States, as they correspond closely with Reports from the Nutrition Committee of the American Heart Association, and the Joint Committee of the US Departments of Health and Human Services, and Agriculture.

ROB SILVERSTONE

The illustrations on the front cover depict the following: spinach roulade (p.91); duckling with honey and lemon (p.111); light 'n' fruity cheesecake (p.126); summer fruit tartlets (p.129).

Introduction

Modern-day France still comprises a large rural population, and this contact with the land is reflected in the nation's cooking habits. Originally the phrase 'table d'hôte' literally referred to a meal derived from the host's own produce, and in French towns and cities many chefs still go early to market to select the best food available and tailor their menus accordingly. Britain, by contrast, as the earliest nation to be urbanised, has become the one most removed from the sources of its diet. Much knowledge relating to the cooking and medicinal qualities of local plants and herbs has long since been lost.

In recent years, however, there has been a resurgence of interest in the connections between food and health, and in several respects nutritional attitudes have undergone a transformation. Traditional guidelines used to centre upon eradicating diseases related to *deficiencies* of certain nutrients. Nowadays, *excessive* intake of certain foods is considered the major area of concern, contributing towards the many diseases of affluence which afflict the Western world.

Recent debates on nutritional policy have been surrounded by controversy and even political involvement. This is, perhaps, not surprising given the vested interest of the food industry and the powerful influence it can bring to bear at the highest level of government. Today, though, despite the polemics, a new consensus has emerged concerning the concept of a healthy diet: overall, the average person would benefit from eating more fresh fruit, vegetables and foods high in natural fibre, and less sugar, salt and saturated fat.

Coincidentally, a number of great chefs have sought to incorporate such nutritional thinking into exquisite forms of cuisine. They have destroyed the image of healthy food as dull, unappetising fare, and won international acclaim for their efforts. Alain Senderens, a famous Parisian chef, encapsulates the rationale behind healthy eating:

> I am obsessed by the relationship between cooking and health. When one goes to the opera one does not expect to return having gone deaf, one does not expect to go blind as a result of going to the theatre. Why

then must one do oneself damage by going out to eat? . . . We must find the means of reconciling pleasure and health. I dream of a cuisine that no longer does any harm (P. Levy, 'Cuisine Penseur', *A la Carte*, Jan. 1986, p. 79).

The trend towards healthy eating has permeated almost every level of the catering and hospitality industry: keep-fit centres offering light brasserie-style menus; Anton Mosimann's 'cuisine naturelle' at 'The Belfry' private dining club in London; school meals programmes which attempt to make healthy eating both appetising and good fun; fast food outlets serving beanburgers, and hotels offering 'health weekends' and alternatives to the traditional fried breakfast.

As caterers you will need to adapt traditional practices to meet the requirements of this expanding health food market. When designing or revamping kitchens, more emphasis should be placed on equipment for steaming, grilling, stir-frying and dry sautéing; less on deep frying. More space should be allocated to fresh food storage, less on freezer cabinets. There is a growing public aversion to foods dependent for their production on pesticides and chemicals, battery farming and confinement of animals.

Consequently you may well need to discover supplies of organic foods, free-range eggs and humanely reared animals. These are some of the considerations the modern caterer will have to assimilate, and this book seeks to provide the informed discussion and practical advice necessary to satisfy an increasingly health-oriented public.

Happy eating!
Healthy eating!

ROB SILVERSTONE

Foreword

Not so long ago, certainly in the 1980s, some chefs thought sauce was tipping a carton of cream into the pan. Healthy cooking like healthy eating is a question of balance. There is a world of difference between a chef who uses just a modicum of cream, a pinch of sugar, to the one who relies on it for all he does. Cream and butters and the other fats serve more to disguise the taste of what we eat than they do to enhance it.

And it is also a question for the cook of seeking out the balance of textures and tastes that can create new dimensions and flavours. The cooking has become more exact as it has become more health-conscious. But the underlying truth has not changed: good food should be food that is good for us.

DREW SMITH
Consumers' Association

Part I
The Issues Relating to
Healthy Eating

1 The Nutritional Shape of a Healthy Diet

This chapter outlines what actually constitutes a healthy diet. The key recommendations of the NACNE and COMA Reports are presented with specific reference to consumption of fats, fibre, sugar and salt.

Recent years have seen dramatic changes in the nature of work. Before the Second World War, the majority of the British population was involved in heavy, manufacturing industry, but, today, new technology has greatly reduced the need for physical labour. Work has become more sedentary in character, and increasingly people will operate from computer terminals at home, so dispensing with the need to travel to and from the office each day.

Whether you view this development with optimism, at the abolition of arduous, routine work, or concern at the enforced idleness of a substantial proportion of the population, the fundamental nutritional implication is the same – people need to expend a good deal less energy in the pursuit of their lives. This of itself would present no problem were energy intake reduced accordingly, but to a large extent this has not been the case. 15 per cent of 16–19-year-olds are overweight, and by the age of retirement this figure has reached 52 per cent.[1] The body cannot cope with this overload, and the strain manifests itself in a number of malaises. As the great Scottish physician Dr Abernethy said, 'one-third of what we eat keeps us alive, the other two thirds keep the doctor alive.'

The health problem is not simply confined to excessive dietary intake, but to the *nature* of that intake. The national diet in the developed world has become increasingly dependent on convenience food products which are typically high in fat, sugar and salt and low in fibre. This chapter will examine each of these four components and explain the part they play in a variety of diet-related diseases.

3

What do the initials NACNE and COMA stand for?
The National Advisory Committee on Nutrition
Education (NACNE) published its Report in September
1983. The aim was to provide clear, simple and
unambiguous guidelines for the general population on
what constitutes a healthy diet.
The Committee on Medical Aspects of Food Policy
(COMA) produced its Report in 1984. Its principal
terms of reference were to investigate the connection
between diet and cardio-vascular disease.
The recommendations of these two Reports form the
basis of current dietary advice.

Fats

Fats are the most calorie-packed of all nutrients: just 100 gm contain
between 800 and 900 kilocalories. The percentage of energy derived from
fat in the diet has in fact risen from 37 percent in the 1950s to 42 per cent
today, so contributing towards the increased incidence of diseases associated with overweight; primarily coronary heart disease (CHD) and
maturity-onset diabetes.[2]

All fats and oils are made up of glycerol and three types of fatty acids:
saturated, monounsaturated and polyunsaturated. It is necessary to outline
the difference between these fatty acids in order to appreciate the most
important area of diet-related illness in this country. A diagrammatic
explanation of the structural difference between each fatty acid is provided
in Appendix I.

Saturated fatty acids are so termed because in their molecular structure
each carbon atom is surrounded by, or 'saturated' with, hydrogen atoms.
The COMA Report was quite clear about the 'strong positive relationship
between the proportion of dietary energy derived from saturated fatty
acids and mortality from coronary heart disease'.[3] Saturates increase total
plasma cholesterol, making the blood 'sticky', and causing lumpy obstructions to form on the arterial walls.

The amount of fat, particularly saturated fat, in the national diet is one
of the principal reasons for the United Kingdom having the highest rate of
premature death and illness from heart disease in the world. The implications of this statistic are enormous. Firstly, in terms of human suffering
which incidentally is borne disproportionately by the poorer classes IV and
V, who have a greater dependence on certain cheap, convenience products
which are typically high in saturates. Secondly, in terms of medical cost; in
1983 the cost of heart disease was put at £420 m a year.[4]

Several countries, such as the United States, Canada, Finland and Australia, have reduced the amounts of total and saturated fat in their diets, producing a dramatic decline in mortality from CHD. The two formative nutritional reports of the 1980s – NACNE and COMA – suggested that the United Kingdom follow suit. NACNE recommends a reduction of fat consumption to 30 per cent of dietary energy, of which only 10 per cent should come from saturates. COMA calls for a more modest reduction, recommending levels of 35 percent and 15 percent respectively.

The main sources of saturated fat in the diet are:

- Dairy fats   – butter, cheese, cream, full-fat milk;
- Meat fats   – beef, lamb, pork, bacon, suet, lard, dripping;
- Processed fats – many margarines and cooking fats, and some blended vegetable oils.

Also watch out for fats that are termed 'hydrogenated'. These are exactly the same as saturated fats, being saturated with hydrogen, and are used in food manufacturing to make products more stable and long-lasting.

Polyunsaturated fatty acids make the blood less viscous, prevent the build-up of obstructions on arterial walls and decrease total plasma cholesterol. Some polyunsaturates, such as linoleic acid and the omega-3 fatty acids, are thought to be especially important in preventing heart disease. Polyunsaturates predominate in many vegetable oils, such as safflower, sunflower, soya and corn oils, and are also present in fish oils. For many years great fish-eating nations, such as the Eskimos and Japanese, were known to enjoy a relatively low incidence of heart disease, and now a fish oil product, 'Maxepa' is actually being prescribed for heart disease patients. Free-ranging animals such as birds and game, are also good sources of polyunsaturates.

Monounsaturated fatty acids were until recently regarded as neutral in their effect upon heart disease, neither causing nor preventing it. However research projects in Holland, the United States and Spain have revealed that 'people who eat a diet high in monounsaturated fats, such as olive oil, have a cholesterol balance as favourable to health as those who eat a diet high in polyunsaturates, or those who have a very low fat diet'.[5]

The research centres upon the connection between monounsaturates and high-density lipoproteins (HDLs). HDLs transport cholesterol from the blood stream to the liver and thereby help prevent the build-up of those substances which block the arteries. It now appears that monounsaturates *raise* the level of HDLs in the blood.

Olive oil contains 73 percent monounsaturates as well as the valuable polyunsaturate linoleic acid, so virgin olive oil can now be savoured for its health-promoting properties as well as for its special culinary appeal. Other oils with a similar high proportion of monounsaturates, but also containing polyunsaturates, are peanut, rapeseed and the exquisitely tasting hazelnut oil.

Fibre

In the sixties, the nutritionist T. L. Cleave claimed that the diseases listed here were caused, in part, by consumption of food which had been refined and condensed to such an extent that its fibre and moisture were no longer present. Today Cleave's work provides a pivotal point of reference for those of us interested in developing a healthy form of cuisine.

Tooth decay
Peptic ulcers
Gallstones
Constipation
Appendicitis
Diverticular
   disease
Bowel cancer
Obesity
Types of eczema
   and allergy
Diseases of the
   circulatory
   system

Fibre is an indigestible form of carbohydrate. Its importance lies in facilitating the smooth passage of food through the digestive tract. In addition, dietary fibre favourably influences blood concentrations of cholesterol and glucose, thereby reducing the incidence of heart disease and diabetes. 'Gummy' fibres, found in oats and beans, appear to have the greatest effect in slowing down the absorption of fat and sugar into the blood.

NACNE recommends a 50 percent increase in fibre consumption, from 20 to 30 gm per day, and the simplest way of achieving this target is to eat more unrefined plant foods – cereals, vegetables, fruits and nuts – and fewer processed products.

The sliced, white loaf provides a good illustration of both the attractive selling points and nutritional shortcomings of refined, convenience foods. It is ready-cut, perfect for making sandwiches and toast, and lacks that nasty habit of going stale overnight. It also lacks up to two-thirds of the fibre found in wholemeal bread, as well as a large proportion of the B vitamins, and the minerals potassium, magnesium and zinc.

A traditional dough simply consists of flour, water, yeast and a little salt. In order to achieve the desired consistency and shelf-life, a convenience loaf also contains an average of 15–16 additives, making British bread 'the most chemically treated in Western Europe'.[6] A growing segment of the population is moving away from such products, on the grounds of both health and taste, and Elizabeth David draws on the prophet Isaiah to ask the poignant question: 'Wherefore do ye spend money for that which is not bread?'[7]

Sugar

Packet sugar is the ultimate refined food, containing no vitamins, minerals or fibre – only calories. The average daily intake of 100 gm carries 400 kilocalories, and because sugar comes in such a densely-packed form, it takes up very litle space inside the digestive tract; to consume the equivalent amount of energy in the form of naturally sweet food, you would, for example, need to pack away 2.5 lb of apples. Lacking any such bulk or fibre, the consumer does not experience feelings of fullness or sated appetite, and so is likely to eat additional food, which leads to problems of overweight.

Britons are gluttons for punishment in this respect, consuming £2330 m worth of confectionery in 1984 – more than the combined value of bread and cereals.[8] Cleave argued that, over a period of 20–40 years, the digestive and circulatory systems become strained by over-consumption of sugar, whereupon the 'Saccharine Disease' manifests itself in many of the ailments outlined above.

In addition, refined sugar has been considered responsible for several psychological disorders associated with roller-coasting blood sugar levels, and for reducing the phagocytic activity of white blood cells, the means by which the body fights off infectious diseases. Professor Yudkin, who has spent years researching the effects of sugar in the diet, wrote that, 'if only a small fraction of what is already known about the facts of sugar were to be revealed in relation to any other material used as a food additive, the material would be promptly banned'.[9] It may come as no surprise that NACNE recommends a 50 per cent reduction in sugar consumption.

A worrying trend has been the increased use of sugar in '*invisible*' form. In the 1930s, the proportion of retail sugar (in packaged form) to that contained in manufactured products was 60 : 40. Today that ratio has reversed to 33 : 66, making it more difficult for the consumer to control his or her level of intake. Furthermore, on food labelling, much sugar masquerades under a variety of guises: sucrose, glucose, dried glucose syrup, molasses, lactose, dextrose and golden syrup. Given this scenario, it would be advisable to reduce the amount of convenience products in cooking, unless they are specifically labelled 'no added sugar'.

The harmful effects of sugar upon health become even more apparent when placed in an historical context. Michael Heasman portrays this succinctly in his excellent report, *One lump or two*:

It seems incredible to consider that today's bag of sugar on the supermarket shelf is dependent on a history which started when colonial powers forcibly shifted millions of people from one continent to another, to produce a commodity to be consumed back in a third continent. At this time, sugar destroyed those who produced it. It is only in the last three decades that a slow, but growing body of opinion now believes that those who consume sugar may also be at risk (M. Heasman, *One lump or two*, Bradford University, 1987, pp. 127–8).

Salt

The role of salt in diet-related disease is not as clear-cut as that of fat, fibre or sugar. However there is a good deal of documented research that demonstrates a fall in blood pressure in response to reduced salt intake. In the light of this, NACNE recommends a 25 per cent drop in consumption, from 12 gm to 9 gm per day.

COMA does not specify a precise reduction in sodium intake but does make the important point that up to 70 per cent of dietary salt is added during manufacture. Consequently it would appear that the amount of salt added in the kitchen, or naturally occurring in food, is relatively insignificant, and the best means of reducing salt intake is to cut down on the proportion of convenience foods consumed.

As already indicated, opinion is still evolving in this area. It may be that chloride rather than sodium emerges as the crucial element; alternatively, it may be a question of equalising sodium and potassium intake, so that the body's delicate electrolyte balance is not put out of equilibrium.

Nutrition is a new science, and some outstanding issues such as these remain to be resolved. However, this should not detract from the great advance represented by the NACNE and COMA Reports; now for the first time, there is general agreement on the fundamental criteria for a healthy diet.

The main recommendations of these two Reports are summarized in Table 1.1. By contrast with previous nutritional advice, little attention is paid to protein. This is because current levels of intake are considered quite sufficient; there merely needs to be a shift in the source of protein, from meat and dairy products to foods of plant origin. Similarly, only limited mention is made of vitamins and minerals, as a varied diet, rich in unrefined carbohydrate, should supply all the vitamins and minerals the body needs. The role of these 'micronutrients' – so-called because of the extremely small amounts in which they occur in food – and the growing practice of taking vitamin 'supplements' will be discussed in Chapter 8.

Table 1.1 Summary of the Principal recommendations of the NACNE and COMA Reports

	NACNE	COMA
Fat	A substantial reduction in dietary fat to 30% of total energy. Saturated fat should represent only 10% of overall energy intake.	A reduction in dietary fat to 35% of total energy, of which only 15% should come from saturated fat. People with an increased risk of heart disease should reduce fat intake to 30% and 10% respectively.
Fibre	A 50% increase in fibre consumption to provide an intake of 30 gm per day. This can be achieved by eating more fruit, vegetables and wholegrain cereals.	An unspecified increase in fibre-rich carbohydrate, principally because of its role in lowering blood cholesterol levels.
Sugar	Reduce sugar intake by half.	No further increase in sugar consumption.
Salt	A 25% decrease in salt intake, to 9 gm per day.	An unspecified reduction in salt intake.
General points	Former dietary advice – which focused on provision of 'protein foods', 'energy foods' and 'protective foods' to prevent diseases of *deficiency* – is now of little relevance to current nutritional thinking'.[10] Today, it is necessary to address the problem of *excessive* intake of certain nutrients. The NACNE proposals seek to establish a standard approach to dietary recommendations for the whole population.	A comprehensive policy, involving government, producers and caterers, needs to be developed on nutritional labelling, so that the public may amend their consumption patterns according to the above recommendations. Equally the Common Agricultural Policy should operate in a way that facilitates such dietary change.[11]

Notes and References

1. Report of The National Advisory Committee on Nutrition Education, p. 10, Health Education Council, 1983 (NACNE Report).
2. Report of the Panel on Diet in Relation to Cardiovascular Disease, Committee on Medical Aspects of Food Policy, para. 3.2.3, HMSO, 1984 (COMA Report).
3. The COMA Report, para. 4.1.2.

4. Various, *'The Lancet'*, 10 Dec. 1983, p. 1351 (re: poverty and CHD); J. Fallows and V. Wheelock, 'The means to dietary change', *Journal of the Royal Society of Health*, October 1983, p. 186 (re: economic cost of CHD).
5. M. Polunin, 'Olives make the heart grow stronger', *Independent*, 9 Feb. 1988, p. 15.
6. H. Wright, 'Swallow it whole', *New Statesman Report*, 1981 p. 16.
7. E. David, *English bread and yeast cookery*, Penguin, 1986.
8. G. Cannon *The Politics of food*, Century, 1987, p. 66.
9. J. Pulling, *Additives: a shoppers' guide*, Hutchinson, 1985, p. 8.
10. The NACNE Report, p. 14.
11. The COMA Report, paras. 1.4.3, 2.6.2 and 2.6.4.

2 Applying Healthy Eating in the Kitchen

This chapter is concerned with the practicalities of implementing healthy eating in a working kitchen. Attention is focused principally on the selection of appropriate ingredients and methods of cookery. First, cooking fats, meat, fish and dairy products are considered with regard to lowering the fat content of dishes. Then cereals, fruit and vegetables are examined as the means of increasing dietary fibre. Finally there is discussion on the various ways of reducing dependence on sugar and salt.

Reducing Fat in the Diet

Cooking Fats: Butter, Margarine, Oils and Lard

Cooking fats represent the largest source of fat in the average British diet, accounting for 36.2 percent of total intake.[1] The quantity used in the kitchen can be greatly reduced by careful selection and modification of cooking methods.

Shallow Frying

The sauteuse need only be lightly brushed with an unsaturated oil, sources of which are described in Chapter 1; there is no need to use large quantities of butter. Ensure that the oil is hot, otherwise the food item will soak it up like a sponge. After cooking, place the food on absorbent kitchen paper, so as to drain off any excess fat.

11

Anton Mosimann recommends using non-stick pans, which enable food to be cooked 'à sec', that is without any fat at all. To compensate for the absence of the tasty, caramelised juices which are produced when sautéing in fat, the food items can be steeped overnight in a flavoursome marinade.

Deep Frying

Deep frying should really be avoided in healthy eating as it involves totally immersing the food in a frying medium. If your customers insist on fried food, there are several procedures that can be allowed. Use an unsaturated oil and avoid the two-stage method of frying whereby the commodity is blanched first and finished later. Chips cooked in this way derive 60 per cent of their calories from fat. It is best to prepare home-made, thickly-cut chips, as these absorb less fat than the frozen variety.[2]

Japanese cuisine is famous for a unique method of frying known as '*tempura*'. A combination of flavoursome vegetable oils is carefully blended and brought to frying temperature. Small morsels of chilled food – seafood, fish, meat or vegetables – are dipped in ice-cold batter and dropped into the frying medium. The impact of the cold food hitting the hot oil causes the batter to blow out into a shell, whilst the food within steams in its own juices. The whole process takes only a few seconds, producing a crisp, tasty product – a far cry from the sad, soggy specimen served up in most 'fish and chip' shops.

Another oriental cooking practice, now quite common in this country, is *stir-frying*. Because only a small quantity of oil is required, and cooking takes place over an extremely short period of time, there is less likelihood of fat absorption. Once again, use an unsaturated oil and make sure it is very hot before commencing the stir-fry.

Roasting

Meat, poultry, game and vegetables should only be basted with a minimum of oil, and the practice of wrapping the food in a waistcoat of fat or bacon should be avoided. Roasting trays should likewise be given just a light brushing over, and if the juices that accumulate at the bottom are to be used as the basis for a sauce or gravy the fat should be carefully skimmed off. Although enclosing the tray with foil in effect part-steams the food, it does provide some protection from the dry convection heat in the oven, so reducing the need for basting.

Grilling

Food items should merely be given a light brush to prevent the surface burning or sticking to the grill. Oily fish have a thin layer of fat beneath the skin which melts on contact with the fierce heat, moistening the flesh and in effect providing a means of self-basting; hence little additional oil is required.

Braising and Stewing

Since the 1950s, Britain has enjoyed an outstanding line of cookery writers, from Elizabeth David and Jane Grigson to Elizabeth Luard and Leslie Forbes. Paula Wolfert's *The Cooking of South West France* belongs to this rich tradition.[3] In it she suggests using pork, duck or goose fat to impart flavour to a dish, then removing the fat pieces, chilling the dish and skimming off the fat. This technique only works with the slow, gentle forms of cookery such as braising and stewing; if the temperature reaches boiling-point the fats will incorporate with the cooking liquor.

Altogether the practice of chilling overnight in the fridge not only provides the best means of visibly removing fat, but also allows for an extension fo what Michel Guérard calls 'cooking by exchange', whereby there is a mutual infusion of flavours in a braised dish, between the main food commodity and the cooking liquor.

Poaching, Steaming and Boiling

Steaming, poaching and boiling are all methods suited to healthy eating, as they require absolutely no fat as a cooking medium. Steaming becomes doubly attractive as there is no cooking liquid for nutrients and flavour to leach out into.

Sauce Thickening

The standard textbook sauce is made using a roux thickening. Sauces and soups produced in this way derive 50 percent of their energy from fat.[4] Over and above the health implications, many modern chefs, particularly exponents of nouvelle cuisine, dispense with roux thickening because it makes for a rather stodgy sauce which coats the palate. Instead they devise light, aerated concoctions based on reductions of stocks and cooking juices.

Alternative thickening agents which involve no use of fat are potato flour, rice flour, arrowroot and vegetable purees. The latter provide a range of combinations as wide as the chef's imagination. The 'Pear and Spinach Roulade' (p. 91) was inspired by a similar combination of fruit and vegetable in a 'Cuisine Minceur' puree.

Egg and butter emulsifications, such as sauce hollandaise, should be avoided because of their incredibly high fat content. Equally, the practice of finishing a sauce with butter – 'monter au beurre' – is inappropriate in healthy cuisine.

Brushing with Butter

A common practice in the kitchen is to brush vegetables with butter prior to service. This greatly increases the fat content of the vegetable dish; for example, steamed cabbage derives absolutely no energy from fat, but when it is brushed with butter the fat content rises to 57 per cent.[5] If the vegetables need to be moistened it is far better to use a little reduced vegetable stock.

Pastrywork

Most pastes, such as puff, sweet and shortcrust, have an extremely high fat content, and researchers working for MacDougalls found it impossible to achieve a tender pastry with a fat content of less than 38 per cent. Because of this, certain celebrated forms of healthy cooking omit pastries altogether. Such an approach tends to limit desserts to variations on fresh fruit, whether salads, purees or sorbets. It could be argued that it is far better to experiment with adapting traditional pastry techniques so that healthy catering may boast the same variety of dishes as its mainstream counterpart. *Remember, the fat content of each component of a diet may vary, so long as the overall proportion of energy supplied by fat does not exceed 30–35 per cent.*

Large fat reductions are possible in all areas of pastry and cake making, and often 'hard' saturated fats like butter can be successfully replaced by unsaturated oils and margarines. There are a number of procedures that can be followed to improve the healthy profile of pastry dishes:

- Use a polyunsaturated margarine. Making shortcrust pastry with Flora margarine and wholemeal flour takes a little getting used to, but is by no means impossible. It requires very little working, owing to the softness of the fat, and benefits from a short rest in the fridge of 30–40 minutes – much longer and the pastry becomes rock-hard and breaks up on rolling.
- Choux pastry can also be made with polyunsaturated margarine and wholemeal flour. A 4 egg mixture containing 100 gm of fat should produce a dozen choux buns, so the amount of fat per portion should not be excessive – providing, of course, the shell is not piped full with cream!! Fromage blanc with roasted hazelnuts makes a pleasant savoury filling, while low-fat set yoghurt with fresh fruit provides a perfectly acceptable dessert.
- The overall amount of pastry in a dish can be reduced by carefully rolling the paste out as thinly as possible, omitting the bottom layer of a pie, or simply using a light pastry case that has been baked blind.
- Strudel pastry appears in the recipe section, both in familiar apfel strudel form and as the packaging for little parcels of salmon with lime. A drop of oil or melted butter can be added to the paste, but really there is no necessity to include any fat at all. This, allied to its transparent thinness, makes strudel pastry an ideal and versatile component in light and healthy cookery.

Meat

Meat provides an excellent source of protein, the B vitamins and iron. However red meat and manufactured meat products are generally high in fat content, of which most is saturated fat (see Table 2.1). The meat commodities in the top half of this table derive most of their energy from fat. For the average person, with an energy requirement of 2400 calories a day, NACNE and COMA recommend a fat intake of 80–90 gm. It can be seen that a generous portion of bacon, sausage roll or lamb chop would account for virtually half that intake in one go. Clearly, the target of 30–35 per cent of dietary energy coming from fat would be very difficult to achieve with a consumption pattern rich in these meat items.

By contrast the poultry, game and offal which feature in the bottom half of the table and in the recipes in Part II, are much leaner. Evidently chefs and caterers can radically reduce the fat content of their menus by careful selection of meat items. The adoption of a few important practices during preparation and cooking would be equally beneficial.

- As much visible fat as possible should be trimmed prior to cooking.
- Stews, stocks, braised and poached dishes should be skimmed during cooking. Chilling overnight will assist in the removal of surface fat.
- Cooking juices intended as the basis for a sauce or gravy should first be skimmed of fat.
- Roast meats should be allowed to baste in their own fat. The layer can be removed prior to carving – and should not be used for crackling!
- Poultry skin can be pricked during cooking to allow fat to escape. Before service the skin should be removed.
- Geese and ducks should be pricked regularly during cooking, to release a great deal of fat. If this is done before the bird is put in the oven, the likelihood is that both skin and flesh will be pierced, leading to loss of nutrients and flavoursome juices. Allow at least 20 minutes in a hot oven before commencing the pricking process. As with poultry, the skin should be removed before plating up.

For years the European Common Agricultural Policy rewarded farmers with guaranteed prices for production of unwanted carcass meat. The 'Intervention Boards' bought up these supplies, regardless of falling demand, and so produced the spectacle of growing European food mountains. There are now moves afoot to rationalise this agricultural system, which in 1988 spent £16 b on surplus food.[6] One enlightened move might be for governments to provide incentives for farmers to rear leaner varieties of livestock – deer, game, free-range birds and poultry – all of which are experiencing rising consumer demand. Currently the United Kingdom imports large batches of frozen rabbit from China. Given the animal's prolific breeding performance, it should not take much of an incentive scheme to establish sufficient supplies of home-grown rabbit.

Table 2.1 A comparison of fat content in various meats and meat products

Food item	Energy, in kilocalories, per 100 gm of the food item	Amount of fat, in grams	Amount of energy derived from fat, in kilocalories	Percentage of energy derived from fat
Forerib of beef	290	25.1	226	78
Sirloin of beef	272	22.8	205	75
Loin chop of lamb	377	35.4	319	85
Leg of lamb	240	18.7	168	70
Loin chop of pork	329	29.5	265	80
Leg of pork	269	22.5	202	75
Back bacon	465	40.6	365	79
Pork sausage	367	32.1	289	79
Sausage roll	479	36.2	326	68
Beefburger	265	20.5	184	69
Pheasant, roast	213	9.3	84	39
Venison, roast	198	6.4	58	29
Rabbit	124	4.0	36	29
Calves' liver	153	7.3	66	43
Chicken liver	135	6.3	57	42
Duck, skin and fat removed during cooking	122	4.8	43	35
Chicken, skin removed	121	4.3	39	32

Note: An explanation of how to translate fat into energy is provided in Appendix II (p. 139)
Source: McCance and Widdowson, *The Composition of Foods*, 4th edn, A. Paul and D. Southgate, HMSO, 1978.

Fish

Fish has been described as 'a totally healthy food'.[7] White fish contains virtually no fat, is easily digested and is full of nutrients. Oily fish contains some highly polyunsaturated fatty acids, as well as providing large amounts of vitamins A and D, both of which may be in short supply during deep mid-winter when their common sources – leafy greens and sunlight – are blighted by the weather.

Too often fish is overcooked, which destroys much flavour, succulence and nutritional value. The fact that fresh fish can be eaten raw testifies to how little cooking it ever requires. In Scandinavia, GRADAVADLAX salmon is marinated and eaten raw, as are *'sushi'* and *'sashimi'* in Japan. The Japanese appreciate that lots of goodness lies beneath the skin and around the bones, and consequently they seldom fillet fish. If filleting is essential, try and use the bones for an accompanying stock or sauce.

There are many ways of cooking fish other than frying. Steaming offers the opportunity to imbue the fish with extra flavour and aroma, by adding herbs or spices to the water at the bottom of the steamer. In *Cuisine Minceur* (Macmillan, 1976), Michel Guérard steams bass on a bed of seaweed, to impart the essence of the sea. Equally, *poaching* allows flavour to be improved by devising a tasty court bouillon, and any fat that surfaces during cooking can be simply skimmed off.

Grilling oily fish requires minimal fat for basting; once again *Cuisine Minceur* offers the novel suggestion of grilling upon a layer of dried fennel branches, over charcoal or an open fire. Finally, baking 'en papillote' or tightly enclosed in foil (as with the mackerel recipe, p. 104) is an ideal low-fat form of cookery where all the flavour is retained in the cooking 'package'.

Milk and Dairy Products

Milk is a rich source of protein and calcium, and also supplies significant amounts of the B vitamins, vitamins A and D, and the minerals potassium, zinc, phosphorus and magnesium. *However unskimmed milk is very high in fat*. There are 22.2 gm of fat in a pint of whole milk, compared with just 0.6 gm in skimmed milk. Fortunately skimmed milk is now readily available, and merely switching from full fat to skimmed milk achieves 80 per cent of the reduction in fat intake recommended by the COMA Report.[8] Table 2.2 reveals a similar disparity in fat content across a range of dairy products.

The recipes in this book hardly use cream in any form, and where hard fatty cheeses such as gruyère or Parmesan are selected for their special flavour, they are used in combination with the less fatty Edam. Similarly Greek yoghurt is used in tandem with low- fat natural yoghurt, in order to

Table 2.2   Comparison of the fat content of various dairy products (fat in gm per 100 gm of the product)

Creams and yoghurts	% fat	Cheeses	% fat
Clotted cream	55	Cream cheese	45
Double cream	48	Lymeswold	37
Whipping cream	40	Stilton	35
Crème fraîche	30	Cheddar	34
Single cream	18	Vegetarian cheddar	33
Soured cream	18	Gruyère	33
Half cream	12	Parmesan	29
'Total' Greek yoghurt	10	Edam	23
Natural low-fat yoghurt	0.75	Curd cheese	12
		Fromage frais	0.4–8
		Cottage cheese	4
		Ricotta cheese	4
		Quark	0–10

Sources: Jane Grigson, 'Curds and Ways', *Observer magazine*, 17 Aug. 1986, p. 34; *Tesco Guide to Nutritional Information*, 1987.

limit overall fat content. For the 'Parslied Chicken' (p. 106), a fresh herb stuffing is made with fromage blanc – a combination of cottage cheese, yoghurt and lemon juice. The stuffing is carefully placed under the skin, so that the flavours permeate the chicken during cooking.

Although health faddists were once cruelly caricatured by Alexei Sayle as 'weaving their own yoghurt', today yoghurt has shed its cranky image and emerged as a regular component of the national diet. It contains all the nutrients of skimmed milk and its bacteria can be useful in combating infections; for example, the lactobacilli found in live yoghurt have been shown to clear up digestive disorders.[9]

When stirred into boiling liquids, yoghurt will curdle. This is avoided in the soup recipes by adding it off the heat, once the soup has cooked. The mixture is then liquidised and gently brought up to service temperature with the yoghurt and soup smoothly combined.

Low-fat yoghurts and cheeses are invaluable in producing healthy desserts, substituting for the traditional double cream, whipping cream and cream cheese. Take care to avoid ready-made fruit yoghurts, most of which are packed with added sugar. It is much better to add fresh fruit to yoghurt yourself.

Eggs

Eggs, like dairy products, contain a whole range of vitamins and minerals, notably vitamins A, D and the B complex, calcium, iodine and iron. The big nutritional question mark concerns the cholesterol found in egg yolk, cholesterol being the substance that builds up in the arteries, causing blockages in circulation. For this reason, much dietary advice has recommended restricting egg consumption to just three to four a week.

However some nutritionists argue that the amount of cholesterol contained in eggs is minimal when compared to that produced by the body in response to consumption of saturated fats. A recent study was conducted at the Radcliffe Infirmary, Oxford, using a sample of the population on a healthy, low-fat, high-fibre diet. The sample was divided in two, one group consuming seven eggs a week and the other only two. At the end of the four-month period, there was no discernible increase in the blood cholesterol levels of participants in the seven-egg group.[10]

Whichever theory proves conclusive, the fat content in egg yolks must preclude excessive consumption. Egg whites, however, are virtually devoid of fat, and many of the receipes in this book use the aeration properties of egg whites both to lighten the finished product and to make the eggs go further.

Increasing fibre in the diet

None of the commodities dealt with so far contain any fibre, and most are major sources of dietary fat. By contrast, foods naturally rich in fibre – cereals, vegetables, pulses and fruit – are relatively low in fat, particularly saturates. Fresh fruit and vegetables in fact provide so little fat that they are excluded from government legislation on fat labelling. There are, of course, the odd exception, such as avocados and nuts, but overall the nutritional profile of plant foods makes them ideal components of a heathy diet.

Cereals

Oats provide such a good source of 'gummy' fibre and B vitamins that it is worth devising ways of using them other than simply for porridge or muesli. Try oats as an ingredient in biscuits, bannocks, crumble topping and stuffings. Barley has a pleasant texture and acts as a good thickening agent for soups and stews, and both barley and oatflakes can be used in bread-making. However the most common cereal for bread and pastry making is wheat flour.

Wholemeal flour is 'the whole grain of the wheat, from which nothing has been extracted and to which nothing has been added'. *Wheatmeal* flour contains 81–90 per cent of the whole grain, and *granary* flour is wheatmeal mixed with malted wheat and rye. There are various other flours available, such as buckwheat, used for blini, a yeast-risen pancake of Russian origin, and cornmeal from maize.

Unrefined flour can be used to produce light crêpes, choux pastries and sponges. Remember to sift the flour first, before returning the bran to the mixing bowl; that way it is lightened without any loss of fibre. Wholemeal flour will never achieve an adequate degree of transparency in filo or strudel pastry, but, as mentioned earlier, it can be used to make good quality shortcrust and choux pastry. It may be easiest to start out with a 50 : 50 combination of white and brown flour, before working towards a higher fibre content. Similarly, experimentation will reveal whether wholemeal or wheatmeal flour is best suited to a particular product.

Elizabeth David uses this approach in bread-making, using either wheatmeal flour or a combination of wholemeal and strong white flour.[11] However avoid being over-cautious with wholemeal flour; apart from the important fibre content, it contributes a great deal of texture and flavour to bread. The wholemeal loaf increased its share of the total bread market from 2 per cent in 1978 to 20 per cent in 1986, and this trend looks set to continue.[12]

Perhaps the whole tradition of buttering bread derives in part from the nature of the convenience white loaf. Its bland, insubstantial character demands a thick coating of some sort in order to provide any semblance of taste. In most European countries bread is appreciated in its own right, accompanying a meal just as it is. Imagine an eating-out experience liberated from those infuriating foil butter portions!

Pasta

Pasta has experienced a rehabilitation as a health food. For many years it was mistakenly regarded as extremely calorific, on account of the rich, creamy sauces that typically accompanied it. In fact, pasta deserves a slim-line profile, 100 gm containing on average just 130 kilocalories. The standard ingredients are strong durum wheat, eggs, water and a little olive oil. Obviously the fat content will vary with the quantity of egg yolks used. Anton Mosimann uses very few in *Cuisine Naturelle* (Macmillan, 1985), while the Time–Life recipe in *The Cooking of Italy* produces a very good paste, using one egg white to each whole egg. However the important thing is not to smother the dish with lots of Parmesan and cream.

Pasta is now available in a great variety of shapes and sizes, as well as in wholemeal form. It is hoped that you will find it both enjoyable and economic to make your own.

Rice

There is a wide choice of grains now available, but *brown rice* is most appropriate because of its high fibre content. It absorbs more liquid and takes longer to cook than other varieties, but there is no need initially to sweat down in fat as the grains tend not to stick together. The flavour can be improved by using fresh stock and herbs in the cooking liquor. Similarly, saffron will impart a subtle golden quality and tumeric a flaming yellow.

Brown rice can also be used successfully in puddings. It must be admitted that the thought of attempting a brown rice peach conde did initially induce some scepticism, but the end-product proved most enjoyable. The recipe came from *Naturally Delicious Desserts* (Faye Martin, Rodale, 1980) now sadly out of print. With the benefit of current nutritional knowledge, the book is clearly lacking in the area of dietary fat – similarly *Cuisine Minceur* somewhat neglects the role of fibre – but we owe a large debt of gratitude to these pioneering healthy cookbooks.

Vegetables and Fruit

In addition to fibre, fruit and vegetables provide a wealth of vitamins. Produce of an orange/yellow hue, such as apricots, melons, carrots and peaches, are generally rich in vitamin A. Good amounts of vitamin C are found in potatoes, peppers, citrus fruit, berries and blackcurrants, while green leafy vegetables contain a whole range of vitamins: A, B_6, folic acid, C, E and K. A comprehensive description of the sources and functions of the various vitamins is provided in Appendix IV (p. 149).

Freshness of produce and minimal preparation are the keys to retaining the nutritional value of fruit and vegetables. Avoid peeling wherever possible: Jerusalem artichokes, new carrots and potatoes only require a good scrub. Elaborate garnishes may produce a spectacular visual effect, but over-handling will reduce vitamin content.

The traditional practice of boiling vegetables in lots of salted water results in loss of colour, flavour and nutrients. Soggy, boiled cabbage epitomised all that was bad about British cookery. The best cooking methods are:

- rapid stir-frying
- steaming
- poaching.

The less liquid used and the shorter the cooking time, the more likely it is that the food will retain its intrinsic qualities. On a visit to Guérard's restaurant at Eugénie-les-Bains, the gourmets Blake and Crewe wrote that 'his vegetables had the superb quality of being cooked, yet tasting as if they were raw'. This is arguably the standard that chefs should seek to emulate.

Guérard poaches vegetables until they are *al dente*, then plunges them into cold running water to arrest the cooking process. Drained, they are crisp and colourful, ready for rapid re-heating at service time. Only French beans are boiled, in order to release the enzyme that would otherwise turn their brilliant green colour a dull khaki.

Pulses and Beans

These are high in fibre, low in fat and so provide a healthy source of protein. Soya beans contain twice the protein of other legumes, with an amino-acid balance approaching that of meat. The protein in soya beans can be extracted to form textured vegetable protein (TVP), but the gastronomic experience of TVP has been compared with 'trying to digest a minced trampoline'. Fortunately new brands, such as Tivall, have been launched, which are much more palatable, the flavour and aftertaste of soya having been removed.[13]

Dried beans and pulses require a good overnight soak in cold water. They should then be drained and rinsed in a colander, before being immersed in fresh water, brought to the boil, and simmered till tender. Do not discard the cooking liquor, as it can be used to improve a soup or stock. The exception is kidney beans, which contain a harmful natural toxin. After soaking, the beans should be boiled for ten minutes, then drained and thoroughly rinsed before being returned to a fresh pan of boiling water for final cooking. On no account should the cooking liquor be used elsewhere.

Beans and pulses are used in a variety of ways in vegetarian cooking. Keith Botsford of *The Independent* suggested a recipe for a Czech bean loaf, using a puree of haricot beans flavoured with nuts, sweetened with honey and lightened with stiff egg whites. The taste was really quite good.

Reducing Sugar in Cooking

Table 2.3 below gives an indication of the surprising amount of sugar contained in manufactured food products. It would make sense for the caterer to substitute sugar-free alternatives for such brands. Perhaps the most disturbing examples are those like bran, muesli and fruit yoghurt, which are perceived by the public as being healthy.

For desserts, naturally sweet foods such as fruit, carob and honey can be used. Sugar in fruit is so diluted with water and fibre that one feels full before eating a significant amount. Honey contains a trace amount of minerals, is lower in kilocalories than sugar (300 as against 400 kilocalories per 100 gm), and is less quickly absorbed into the bloodstream. However it is by no means the mystical wonder food portrayed in some health books and should only be consumed in moderation. Nowadays there is a wide selection of honeys available, carrying the subtle essence and aroma of the blossoms from which they originate – rose petal, lime, lavender and so on. If the taste of honey is off-putting, try the acacia variety, as it provides sweetness without the distinctive honey flavour.

With demand for sugar falling, the race is on to produce the consummate sugar substitute. *Sorbitol* and *fructose* are refined carbohydrates with a similar energy content to sugar; consequently they are of little health

Table 2.3   The sugar content of various food products

Food item	Sugar in gm per 100 gm
Meringue nests	93
Blackcurrant drink	72
Redcurrant jelly	63
Strawberry jam	62
Sugar puffs	56
Chocolate	43
Mushroom soup (dried)	33
Sweet pickle	30
Muesli	26
Bran flakes	17
Apricot yoghurt	13
Tomato ketchup	11
Canned peaches in syrup	10

Sources: Michael Heasman, *One lump or two*, Bradford University, May 1987, p. 56; *Tesco Guide to Nutritional Information*, 1987.

value, either in general terms or specifically in relation to diabetes.[14] A new product, *Xylitol*, has the same sweetness and calories as ordinary sugar, but does not cause tooth decay and can be used by diabetics as it is metabolised independently of insulin.

The British Diabetic Association recommends the use of two low-calorie substitutes, *saccharine* and *aspartame*. The latter, more commonly known as Candarel or Nutrasweet, is employed enthusiastically by Michel Guérard in *Cuisine Minceur*: 'Increasingly synthetic sugars are of a remarkable quality, and allow us to produce results, especially in pâtisseries, which are really quite astonishing'.[15] Undoubtedly, Candarel has been a massive money-spinner for G. D. Searle, the company that developed it and, not surprisingly, Tate and Lyle are hot on their tail, devising a new calorie-free sweetener, *sucralose*.

Although sugar substitutes undergo stringent tests before being passed as fit for consumption, some doubts have been raised concerning their effects on health. For this reason, none appears in the dessert recipes that follow in line with Anton Mosimann's view that artificial sweetening is unnatural: 'I don't believe in it and I never use it'.[16]

Reducing Salt in Cooking

The principal sources of salt in the diet are convenience products, particularly dried stocks, soups and sauces. Consequently salt consumption can be significantly reduced by moving from convenience to fresh foods. In *Cuisine Naturelle*, Anton Mosimann goes further than this, rarely seasoning with salt and instead using combinations of herbs to produce additional flavour.

By contrast, Michel Guérard seasons normally, as he does not wish *Cuisine Minceur* dishes to be bland. Additionally, in rather an original way, he sometimes uses salt as a cooking utensil rather than a flavouring. For example, chicken is cooked in a cake of moist salt; where the salt no longer acts as an element which flavours, but as a crust which crystallises on heating, and which forms a type of oven, a second oven, in which the chicken is simply cooked. A novel form of enclosed cookery is created – similar to 'en croûte', 'en papilotte' and today's technological equivalent, 'sous-vide' – whereby the food item is entirely sealed, preventing the escape of juices and nutrients.

Salt substitutes are now widely available, most of them being combinations of sodium chloride and potassium chloride. Such products may be especially useful when catering for the elderly, who might otherwise add excessive amounts of salt to their food in order to compensate for loss of taste sensation. A new substitute is being developed in the USA, derived from strains of food yeasts, which is low in sodium and potassium, and is claimed to have a 'very convincing' salt flavour.[17]

Notes and References

1. V. Wheelock and J. Fallows, *Implications of the COMA Report for British agriculture*, Bradford University Food Policy Research Unit, 1985, p. 12.
2. J. Hill *et al.*, 'Low-fat chips', *Nutrition and Food Science*, July 1984, p. 8.
3. P. Wolfert, *The Cooking of South West France*, Dorling Kindersley, 1987, pp. 12–14.
4. P. Scobie, 'Catering for Health', *Nutrition and Food Science*, Sept. 1987, p. 18.
5. Ibid.
6. D. McKenzie, 'The mystery of the mountains', *The Food Magazine*, vol. 1, no. 1, p. 7.
7. J. Rogers, *The Taste of Health*, BBC pub., 1985, p. 38.
8. Ibid., *The Coma Report*, para. 5.4.
9. M. Downall, 'Yoghurt: an old cure', *Independent*, 24 May 1988, p. 17.
10. H. Fore, 'Eggs', *Nutrition and Food Science*, July/Aug. 1988, p. 16.
11. E. David, *English bread and yeast cookery*, Penguin, 1986, p. 256.
12. Anon, 'Food Facts' *Nutrition and Food Science*, March/April 1987, p. 18.
13. C. Spencer, 'Kibbutzburgers and spring buds', *Guardian*, 12 March 1988, p. 23.
14. Various, *Dietary recommendations for diabetics in the 1980's*, British Diabetic Association, 1983.
15. Interview with the author at Eugénie-les-Bains, Sept. 1985.
16. Interview with the author at The Dorchester, October 1985.
17. G. Cannon and C. Walker, *The Food Scandal*, Century, p. 208.

3 Obtaining Quality Supplies of Wholefoods

When implementing a nutritious diet, it is advisable to obtain supplies that are in prime, unadulterated condition. This approach is best reflected in two important trends: first, the means by which caterers seek to obtain the freshest produce possible; second, the increase in demand for organic foods, which have been cultivated or reared without recourse to chemicals.

Access to fresh, local produce

Most large wholesalers and catering suppliers now carry stocks of basic healthfoods, such as dried pulses and wholemeal flour. Less common products, such as tofu or couscous, can usually be obtained from the multitude of health shops that have sprung up throughout the country, or direct from the distributors that supply them. Whatever the source of supply, it is best to retain a critical outlook. For example, a pint of soya milk – ostensibly a wholesome Vegan alternative to dairy milk – could quite possibly contain various forms of added sugar and a whole list of preservatives and flavourings.

Both in terms of taste and nutritional value, it makes sense to purchase foods that are as fresh as possible. Unfortunately it is not uncommon to sit down to a meal in a seaside town in Britain and be presented with a sad, lacklustre fish that has evidently journeyed all the way to Billingsgate and back. Similarly, many vegetables imported from France arrive in better condition than those originating from British farms. Alan Porter, who supplies fruit and vegetables to top restaurants and country house hotels, realises that this is a sorry state of affairs.

We should use our own raw materials. Chefs should understand the product they have on their doorstep. They should do something with it. They should be creative . . . [too many chefs] live off some creator in another country. They do not use their own imaginations. That is the

25

problem. They use someone else's thoughts. And they pay big money
to find the ingredients that another person has created a dish from.[1]

Since he made this comment, in 1986, things have improved a good deal. A
new wave of talented chefs has emerged whose cuisine is characterized by
dependence on local produce. A growing number of restaurateurs and
hoteliers now deal direct with the farmer. This ensures absolute freshness,
as well as precision in specification of size and quality. Just as some small
farmers are now forming consortia to reach a wider public, so chefs are
linking up, to give themselves greater buying influence with the growers.
The 'Grow for it!' campaign, launched jointly by *Caterer and Hotelkeeper*
magazine and the National Farmers Union, epitomised the movement to
develop local contacts between farm and kitchen.

A number of country hotels are going one step better and growing their
own herbs, fruit and vegetables, utilising what had hitherto been a fallow
acre or two of land. Obviously there is a cost equation to be made between
the wages of gardeners and savings from food deliveries, but the benefits in
terms of quality and flavour are undisputable. The garden at Raymond
Blanc's 'Manoir aux Quatr' Saisons', bears ample witness to this.

On a more modest scale, catering students attempted to implement these
practices in the kitchen at Dorset Institute of Higher Education. Early one
May, when the markets and greengrocers generally languish in the hiatus
between winter and summer crops, they ordered the first of the new
season's produce from Mersley Farm on the Isle of Wight. The leafy shoots
of the carrots were sappy and bright and the asparagus lay plump and
proud. They selected the best of the day's catch from Talbot Fisheries, who
are supplied by a local fishing vessel, and collected fresh herbs from the
little patch nurtured by storeman Sid. The resulting meal was simple, but a
real treat for the tastebuds.

There is really no reason why prime, fresh products should be considered the exclusive preserve of up-market catering. Changes in Common
Market agricultural policy will remove the incentive to cultivate vast fields
of cereals, and farmers may have to diversify into supplying the needs of
the caterer, in order to survive.

Freshness alone is not a guarantee of the wholesomeness of produce. In
recent years there has been growing concern about the amount of
chemicals used in conventional farming, and consequently the demand for
organically raised crops and livestock has risen dramatically.

The Rationale for Organic Farming

After the Second World War, modern farming technology was heralded as
an economic miracle that would maximise the productivity of the land and
provide a solution to world hunger. Unfortunately that utopian vision has
turned into something of an ecological nightmare. The prairie-type fields

which now dominate much of the British landscape were created by tearing up 120 000 miles of hedgerow and over one-third of ancient woodland. Dependence on chemical fertilizers has depleted the organic matter in the soil which acts as a vital binding agent. This, allied to the removal of the hedgerows, has led to soil erosion by wind and rain.

Nitrates from fertilisers are now accumulating in the water supply. The World Health Organization limit for nitrate in drinking water is 11.3 mg per litre, yet in Britain levels of 15–20 mg per litre are fairly typical in sources below arable fields. Current nitrate contamination of drinking water relates back to fertilisers applied twenty years ago, so the full penalty for today's more intensive chemical agriculture will be paid by future generations. Farm slurry, or the excreta from confined animals, is a further source of contamination. The slurry is pumped into lagoons, which inevitably leak, infecting nearby land and waterways. In 1984 the Ministry of Agriculture was notified of 3000 incidents of pollution caused in this way.[2]

Apart from the damage in terms of conservation, modern farming technology has not created a particularly effective system. Insecticides have not reduced the incidence of pests, as they kill the creatures which are their natural predators, and promote the growth of super-pests, which develop resistance to the chemicals. In the USA, crop losses from pests have risen from 7 per cent in the 1940s, to 13 per cent now, despite a tenfold increase in the use of insecticides.[3]

Intensive agriculture has produced vast food surpluses, which cost the EC (European Community) an estimated £16 b in 1988. Significantly, the 20–25 per cent fall in output that accompanies a conversion from conventional to organic methods is virtually equivalent to the current level of overproduction. The whole costly business of subsidies, guaranteed prices and storing surpluses could be removed by reverting to organic farming.[4]

The intensive rearing of livestock has attracted much criticism on the grounds of inhumane treatment. Although the veal crate system, whereby calves were closely penned for several months, has now been banned, most pigs and poultry are raised in similarly confined conditions. Two-thirds of home-produced pork and bacon derive from the 'dry sow' or 'tether stall' close confinement systems. The aim is to produce a super-efficient sow, with five pregnancies in two years, but the cost in terms of animal welfare is considerable.

> I recently visited a set of pig units. The five long sheds with shuttered tin ventilators housed 4,000 pigs, You could smell the stench a mile away. The units are mostly airless, and for most of the time in complete darkness. The pigs stand or lie in their own excreta, slumped in dejection, their only movement to chew bar, tether or chain . . . When first tethered, all pigs undergo intense activity. They turn, twist and thrash their heads. They emit loud screams and throw their whole body to the floor and sides of the stall. On average they spend 45 minutes in

grotesque pain. The escape reaction is followed by days of inactivity. They are completely immobile for long periods, occasionally punctuated by another escape reaction, straining at the tether or trying to bite through the bars (Colin Spencer, 'Life of the pig in our green and pleasant land', *Guardian*, 23 Jan. 87, p. 18).

In order to counteract the stress induced by such living conditions, some rearers inject their animals with tranquillisers. These are not the only little extras on offer. Certain antibiotics are routinely added to animal feeds, to reduce the incidence of infection, and hormones and anabolic steroids are used to boost the growth rate of young animals. Following the appearance of growth-promoting hormone residues in animal flesh, and concerned for the effect on human health, the EC has decided to ban them. However, in the absence of any effective policing of farm drugs, the ban is likely to prove rather meaningless.

How is Organic Farming Different?

The government has set up a Ministry of Agriculture, Fisheries and Food (MAFF) working party to establish nationwide standards for organic production methods. Until such time as it reports, the Soil Association (SA) remains the principal guardian for organic farming. It allows

- no artificial fertilisers
- no synthetic sprays
- no feed additives
- no permanent penning, caging or tethering of livestock.

Crops are only given the SA seal of approval once all traces of chemical residue have disappeared from the soil; and in order to carry their symbol for organic meat, the livestock must be naturally raised on organically grown grass and dry feed.

Instead of segregating pastoral and arable production, organic farming combines the two to good effect. Animal manures, clover and compost are used as natural fertilisers and the system of crop rotation further enriches the soil. For three or four years the land is kept under grass for pasture, and the resultant fertility supports cereal or vegetable crops for the next couple of years. In place of pesticides, certain insects and fungi are used to control specific pests, but generally the spread of disease is discouraged by the system of crop rotation, and the vitality of a naturally healthy soil.

As far as possible, livestock are allowed to feed and exercise freely. Contrast the confined pig farm described earlier with the methods of the Youngs in the Cotswolds, who graze their cattle in extended family groupings, and know each of their herd by name. Cattle on the Young farm live to 20 years of age – 3 times the national average.[5]

The Soil Association symbol

Many people testify to the incomparable flavour of organic meat, and there is also evidence to suggest that it is nutritionally superior. Alan Gear, author of *The New Organic Food Guide* (Dent, 1987) explains:

A typical modern carcass may contain 25–30% fat and only 50–55% lean. This fat runs throughout the meat. On the other hand, a cow free to select its own feed and range over the land has been shown to have only 3.9% of carcase fat, and a lean tissue mass of 79%. Furthermore, the tendency is for the fat to be concentrated in an outer layer which can be cut off. This enormous difference in the proportion of fat to lean inevitably invites speculation as to whether it is not modern farming methods which are causing the problems, rather than there being anything intrinsically unhealthy about meat itself.

Alan Gear's book includes a comprehensive directory of organic growers up and down the country. Despite the increase in farmers operating under Soil Association standards, the home market cannot keep up with escalating demand. Consequently 60–75 per cent of organic food sold in Britain is imported. The situation would be improved if the Ministry (MAFF) were to offer advice on how to go about converting from traditional methods, and provide incentives for going organic.

To meet the shortfall in supply, several organisations have emerged whose standards are much looser than those set by the SA. For example, the Guild of Conservation Food Producers, whose products carry the 'Conservation Grade' symbol, do not actually embrace organic farming methods. Instead they avoid the worst excesses of intensive farming, by limiting the use of chemicals, raising cattle without recourse to antibiotics or growth promoters, and abiding by an animal welfare code.

Notes and References

1. Drew Smith, 'The Gourmet Wagon . . .', *Guardian*, 5 Sept. 1986, p. 12.
2. Alan Gear, *The New Organic Food Guide*, Dent, 1987, pp. 15–17.
3. Ibid, p. 10.
4. J. Richard, 'Organic food . . . ', *Guardian*, 25 July 1986, p. 16.
5. V. McKee 'Animal Farm', *Guardian*, 4 July 1987, p. 21.

Additional Recommended Reading

Organic
Cunningham, J., 'Getting the drift', *Guardian*, 27 Feb. 1987, p. 18.
Jones, J., 'Organic farming may win EC subsidies', *Independent*, 28 Feb. 1989, p. 6.
Spencer, C., 'The taste of a bitter earth', *Guardian Weekend*, 4 Feb. 1989, p. 11.
Various, 'Food adulteration and how to beat it', *London Food Commission*, Unwin, 1988.

Supplies fresh from the producer
Rounds, J., 'No frills . . . ', *Independent*, 29 Apr. 1989, p. 34.
Till, C., 'Everything in the garden', *Chef*, October 1986, p. 11.
'Grow for it' campaign, *Caterer and Hotelkeeper*, issues 10, 17, 24 July 1986.

4 The Nutritional Effects of Food Processing

This chapter outlines the nutritional effects of food
technology as manifested in the following systems:
canning, freezing, chilling, sous-vide and irradiation. It
then goes on to explore the controversy surrounding the
use of additives in the food manufacturing process.

Ideally, meals should be comprised of predominantly fresh produce, but
processed foods also have an important role to play in the provision of a
healthy diet. For example, pulses, beans and pasta – all of which are now
appreciated for their low fat/high fibre content – are widely available,
thanks to the processes of drying and canning.

Before considering the effects of various systems of preservation on the
nutritional quality of food, it should be acknowledged that certain nutrients are also depleted when fresh foods are cooked conventionally. This
is especially the case when food is overcooked, or left in water or daylight
for long periods prior to cooking. The essential point, though, is that,
starting with fresh foods, the caterer can operate in such a way as to retain
the maximum intrinsic qualities of food. When starting with processed
foods, some of these properties will already have been lost.

Canning

Canned products have in effect been cooked twice before they reach the
consumer. First they are blanched in order to inactivate enzymes which
would cause the food to produce gas, soften and discolour. Peas, for
example, are blanched for six minutes at 95°C, resulting in a 36 per cent
loss of vitamin C, 30 per cent of vitamin B_2 and 16 per cent of vitamin B_1.[1]

Then, once the can has been hermetically sealed, the food is sterilised by
a further application of heat, which in the case of peas is 14 minutes at

121°C. Consequently a vegetable which ordinarily would require a gentle poaching for five minutes, is subjected to 20 minutes at a much higher temperature, resulting in degradation of heat-labile nutrients such as vitamin B_1. Further loss may occur during storage as nutrients leach into the canning liquid, but this may be compensated by using the liquid for stocks and soups.

Freezing

Most foods are blanched prior to freezing, but the principal factor determining nutrient loss is the speed at which the food is brought down to − 18°C. If this process is protracted, ice crystals will form within the cell structure and melt upon defrosting, draining away vitamins, minerals, proteins and peptides. Long-term storage of up to a year will result in some additional nutrient loss, but, overall, freezing is considered one of the best methods of preserving vitamins and other nutrients.

In the mid-1960s, the idea developed of harnessing the benefits of freezing to large-scale catering operations. A pilot study was conducted in Leeds between 1967 and 1972, aimed at supplying the local school meals service. Under this *cook–freeze* system, food was prepared and cooked in bulk, portioned and then blast frozen. The dishes were stored at − 18 to − 20°C, before being distributed for regeneration as required.

Some delicate dishes, such as egg custards and soft fruits, were not suitable for cook–freeze, and modified starch had to be added to sauces in order to prevent them separating. Altogether, though, this new development in food technology proved very successful, and it was widely applied in welfare and institutional catering. The system of one large central production unit supplying several peripheral outlets enabled substantial cost savings to be made through bulk purchasing, rationalisation of kitchen staff and maximum utilisation of equipment.

Cook–chill

During the 1980s cook–freeze was largely displaced by *cook–chill*, principally because of the lower energy costs involved in chilling rather than freezing foods. Dishes are blast chilled to a temperature between 0 and 3°C, and held there for a maximum of five days. By keeping the holding temperature above freezing-point, all food commodities can be used and very few modifications, if any, are necessary to standard recipes.

It has been claimed that the taste and vitamin retention of cook–chill dishes are superior to those produced by alternative systems, but in reality there is little evidence to support this claim. One of the few substantial research studies into cook–chill, conducted in Germany in the late 1970s, revealed a sharp decrease in palatability after just three days, and a substantial loss of vitamin C; cook–chilled vegetable and potato dishes were found to contain between 30 and 90 per cent less ascorbic acid than their freshly prepared equivalents.[2]

Although cook–chill is meant to replace the old practice of warm-holding food, in some ill-conceived operations chilled food is regenerated centrally and then distributed under warm-held conditions. This combines the nutritional disadvantages of both cook–chill and conventional methods. Additionally, if inaccurately monitored for temperature, warm-holding provides ambient conditions for the multiplication of bacteria.

Current concern surrounding cook–chill relates precisely to this issue of bacterial contamination. Originally it was considered safe to store foods for five days under chilled conditions, because bacteria would scarcely grow below 3°C. Now Professor Richard Lacey of Leeds University has highlighted two strains of bacteria which grow quite rapidly at these low temperatures: listeria and yersinia. Listeria can survive short cooking above 65°C, to multiply when chilled. Professor Lacey attributes three times as many deaths per year to listeria as salmonella poisoning. Yersinia does not survive cooking above 65°C, but can also readily multiply under chilled conditions.[3]

It would appear that, in the interests of healthy eating in the widest sense, cook–chill systems:

- should operate under the strictest hygienic control, ensuring that food is cooked *thoroughly* at temperatures above 65°C, then rapidly chilled to below 3°C, before final regeneration at a temperature capable of killing off bacteria;
- should not be assembled piecemeal, incorporating some of the less satisfactory features of conventional practice, but should be implemeted as logically flowing, complete systems;
- should be subject to more detailed research with regard to the retention or loss of particular nutrients.

These suggestions deserve urgent attention, particularly as cook–chill is being widely taken up by district health authorities. Hospital patients are more susceptible to food poisoning, given their weakened condition, and require a nutritious diet, rich in vitamins in order to facilitate a speedy recovery from illness, surgery and mental stress.

Sous-vide

Sous-vide also uses chilling as a means of holding food. Invented in France in the 1960s, by George Pralus, it has recently attracted much interest in Britain. Sous-vide is based upon the ancient principle of enclosed cookery, whereby the juices of a commodity are sealed within a vessel. In medieval times small birds were placed inside larger ones, in Scotland a sheep's stomach is used to enclose the ingredients for a haggis, and in *haute cuisine* a similar result is achieved by tightly wrapping food 'en papillote'.

New technology advances this principle one stage further by enclosing food within a laminated plastic cryovac bag. The food item is placed carefully inside the bag, which is then evacuated of air and heat-sealed in a vacuum-packing machine. Cooking then proceeds in a steam convection oven at a relatively low temperature: approximately 100°C. Once cooked, the food is rapidly chilled to between 0 and 3°C, and can be stored for up to eight to ten days.[4]

There are many advantages to this system. Low temperature cooking avoids the denaturation of connective tissue which causes toughness in meat, and dramatically reduces the shrinkage of joints of meat: from 25–35 per cent in normal roasting to 2–8 per cent with sous-vide. Enclosing in the sealed bag carries several benefits: firstly, food can be rapidly chilled by immersion in an ice bath; secondly the contents are safe from cross-contamination during storage; and thirdly all the flavour is imprisoned within the bag. Using conventional methods, a certain amount of goodness inevitably leaches out into the cooking medium, but with sous-vide there is no possible means of escape. Logically, sous-vide should be equally effective in retaining nutrients, but as yet there has been minimal research into the nutritional effects of cooking in the bag and the lengthy storage period.

Recent concern relating to the bacterial contamination of cook–chilled food has revealed that listeria, yersinia and botulinum can also survive inside vacuum packs. Consequently it is essential that the internal temperature within the pouch is sufficient to destroy bacteria. In France, successful attendance at the Pralus training course is compulsory before a licence is granted to operate sous-vide systems. It could be argued that similar control should be exercised in Britain, encompassing all centralized production systems.

Irradiation

One quite controversial means of containing bacterial contamination is food irradiation. Several sources of spoilage can be destroyed by subjecting food to varying levels of ionising radiation:

- Radurisation, which generates a dose 100 times greater than a chest X-ray, inhibits the sprouting of vegetables, delays the ripening of fruit and kills off pests in grains, spices and fruit.
- Radicidation reduces the incidence of yeasts, moulds and bacteria, so extending the shelf-life of products.
- Radappertisation completely sterilises food, killing all bacteria and viruses.

There are numerous serious criticisms of this form of food processing:

1. Irradiation severely damages vitamins, particularly A, C, D, E, K and some of the B complex.
2. Milk and fats do not irradiate well, developing what has been described as a 'wet dog' smell.
3. Although it is claimed that the process would enable a reduction in chemical food additives, an equivalent number of additives would in fact be required to control some of the undesirable effects of irradiation.
4. The suggested level of food irradiation would destroy the yeasts and moulds that are the natural competitors of botulinum, the bacteria that causes botulism, without being strong enough to kill the botulinum itself.
5. Not enough is known about the effect on human health resulting from long-term consumption of irradiated food. Experiments on animals have revealed instances of reduced growth, kidney damage and increased production of aflatoxins – the powerful agents connected with liver cancer.[5]

In 1988, following widespread public opposition, the government shelved plans to legalise food irradiation. However some politicians view irradiation as an easy answer to the growing problem of food poisoning in the United Kingdom, and this has led to the ban being lifted. This response could actually compound the danger to public health. It would be far better to tackle the *causes* of food poisoning, by increasing the resources available to environmental health officers, and making hygiene education more accessible to farmers, food manufacturers and caterers alike.

The criticisms of certain aspects of centralised food production have not been made out of some romantic attachment to a rustic past. New developments in food technology hold great potential for improving the national diet, but they need to be carefully researched and monitored, as the implications of a bad system are so far-reaching. Nestlé are pioneering a process, employing new microwave technology and pasteurisation techniques, which produces dishes that the gourmet Paul Levy considers to be tastier and more innovative than sous-vide products. Additionally, they are virtually free from bacterial contamination; after three days the food contains only 10–50 micro-organisms per gram as compared with 10–20 000 in a competitor's comparable product.[6] Should this system prove to have no adverse effect on nutritional content, then new technology will have developed the means of providing appetising and wholesome meals, available to a wide public.

The Food Additives Debate

The whole issue of food additives has aroused great concern amongst the British public; Maurice Hanssen's paperback *E for Additives* (Thorsons, 1987) sold half a million copies in its first edition and, in a recent survey, 79 per cent of consumers expressed a preference for additive-free food.[7] However not all nutritionists share this level of concern. Verner Wheelock, of Bradford University's Food Policy Research Unit, believes that the dangers of additives have been magnified out of proportion. To support this view, he draws on research which places food additives at the bottom of a list of food safety hazards.[8]

	1	Foodborne hazards of microbiological origin
Descending	2	Nutrition/malnutrition
order of	3	Environmental pollutants
importance	4	Natural toxins (such as solanine in potatoes)
	5	Pesticide residues
	6	Food additives

The inference is that, while the role of additives should not be ignored, the health risk they present needs to be placed in some kind of perspective. Concentration on the additives issue should not detract from the priority areas of establishing safe and hygienic kitchen practice and disseminating basic nutritional education.

Almost inevitably, much attention has focused on the link between additives and cancer, yet a major study by Doll and Peto considers tobacco (30 per cent) and diet (35 per cent) to be the principal causes of cancer, with additives ascribed a very marginal role ($-$ 5 per cent to 2 per cent).[9] The minus 5 per cent factor relates to the possibility that some food additives, in particular preservatives and anti-oxidants, could actually have a protective effect and so be responsible for a reduction in the incidence of cancer. The plus 2 per cent factor is connected with the uncertainty surrounding the use of nitrates.

Nitrates are added to foods such as bacon and meat products in order to guard against botulism. They are broken down into nitrates in the body, and the concern is that they might interact with amines from food in the stomach, to form carcinogenic nitrosamines. Verner Wheelock considers the risk of botulism to be far greater than that of cancer, as the nitrate derived from consumption of cured meat is a fraction of the amount naturally occurring in humans.

Consumer distrust of additives can be explained in part by the confusing series of numbers used to identify them. As a result, harmless additives, such as anti-oxidant E300, which is in fact Vitamin C, will probably be regarded with as much suspicion as the genuinely dubious dye, E102 tartrazine. Many retailers and catering suppliers now provide a range of additive-free lines; perhaps they should also produce information in leaflet form simply describing and categorising the various additives: then consumers would be in a position to make a more informed choice. Appendix III (p. 140) reproduces some useful material made available by the Soil Association.

A good deal of public concern relates to the regulation of food additives. Only 10 per cent of additives are controlled by the system of 'permitted lists', and fewer still have to be declared on food labels. The controls that do exist in the United Kingdom are relatively weak, allowing the use of many additives that have been banned elsewhere.[10] For example:

- Anti-oxidant BHT (Butylated Hydroxytoluene, E321) used extensively in large-scale baking processes, was recommended for withdrawal by a government preservatives sub-committee as long ago as 1963. It has the effect of raising blood cholesterol levels, and may also break down body stores of Vitamin D. BHT is still in use.[11]
- The colouring Amaranth (E123) has been banned in the USA and the Soviet Union because of its cancer-forming quality, and damage incurred to liver and sex organs during tests on animals.
- The Benzoates (E210–E219) and the colouring tartrazine (E102), were shown to provoke hypersensitivity in four out of five children tested at Great Ormond Street Hospital, causing reactions such as asthma and eczema.[12]
- The United Kingdom approves a greater number of artificial food colours than almost any other industrialised country. It allows 17 colours as against 7 in the USA and one in Norway.[13]

The system of safety testing may be inappropriate as additives are only tested singly, when in reality they are consumed in combination. The food campaigner Caroline Walker presented Margaret Thatcher with a Christmas hamper whose goodies contained 170 chemical additives. Such 'cocktails' of additives may react with each other and with food to produce new chemicals. Melanie Miller of the London Food Commission believes it would be extremely time-consuming and expensive to determine the effects of these various chain reactions upon health. It would make more sense simply to reduce the amount of additives used.

Additives are often passed as safe on the basis that they will only be consumed in tiny quantities. This may well be a false premise as the use of additives increased tenfold between 1955 and 1985.[14] It is estimated that each person now eats about 8–11 pounds of additives a year, and this figure is set to double by the end of the century. A survey of takeaway foods in the West Midlands found that 100 per cent of Chinese and Indian meals contained monosodium glutamate, all fish and chip shop batter included artificial colour and less than half the chip samples were without added colour.[15] Clearly those groups of the population which regularly eat 'fast food' are unlikely to consume the minimal amounts of additives which some nutritionists believe to be the norm.

The principal justification for using additives in large-scale food production is that they extend the shelf-life of the product. However there is no inherent necessity to operate in this way; Marks and Spencer run a perfectly efficient distribution and retail system based on selling short-life foods. Perhaps the central rationale for the use of additives is that they enable manufacturers to transform cheap, unappetising ingredients into acceptable products:

> Colours, flavours, texture modifiers and adhesives can be used to turn waste animal material, such as ground up rind and fat, into something resembling acceptable meat . . . You can now take any protein you want, cotton seed or peanut or fishmeal, purify it, dissolve it in alkali, extrude it through tiny holes, wind it up like a great hank of wool and lo and behold you have beef, mutton, turkey or smoked salmon, according to the flavour you care to give it that day (Melanie Miller, *Danger – Additives at Work*, p. 26).

Notes and References

1. S. Holdsworth, *The preservation of fruit and vegetable products*, Macmillan, 1983, p. 133.
2. J. Sheppard, *The Big Chill*, *London Food Commission*, 1987, p. 53.
3. S. de Bruxelles, 'Food poisoning plague', *Observer*, 28 Aug. 1988, p. 9.
4. M. Light *et al.*, 'A pilot study on the use of sous-vide', *International Journal of Hospitality Management*, vol. 7, no. 1, 1988, p. 21.
   B. Whitehall, 'Sous-vide: All systems go', *Caterer and Hotelkeeper*, 23 July 1987, p. 48.
5. T. Webb, 'Food irradiation in Britain', *London Food Commission Report*, September 1985, pp. 10–23.
6. P. Levy, 'A taste of technology', *The Observer Magazine*, 2 Mar. 1986, p. 58.
7. Anon, 'Healthy diet rivals price', *The Grocer*, 12 Oct. 1935, p. 9.
8. V. Wheelock, *Food Additives in perspective*, Bradford University Food Policy Research Unit, Aug. 1986, p. 64.
9. Ibid., p. 51.
10. M. Miller, 'Danger: additives at work', *London Food Commission*, Dec. 1985, pp. 1, 134–9.
11. H. Wright, 'Swallow it whole', *New Statesman Pub*, 1983, p. 17.
12. J. Pulling, 'Additives: a shoppers' guide', Hutchinson 1985, p. 4.
13. M. Miller, 'Danger', p. 15.
14. Ibid, p. 8.
15. Anon, *The Food Magazine*, vol. 1, no. 1, Spring 1988, p. 4.

5 Movements Associated with Healthy Eating

> There are many movements that have contributed
> towards the emergence of healthy eating – spiritual,
> religious, social and ecological. This chapter
> concentrates on the two trends of most direct relevance
> to the caterer; vegetarianism and nouvelle cuisine.

Vegetarianism

The vegetarian ideal dates from ancient times. In Plato's *Republic*, the workers were all vegetarian, and in Plutarch's essay on flesh eating, he defies meat eaters to kill their own food, and speaks of a dinner table 'spread with the mangled forms of dead bodies'. Pythagoras was said to have tamed a bear by introducing it to a vegetarian diet, but he is better known for his powerful statement on the virtues of vegetarianism;

> My fellow men, do not defile your bodies with sinful foods. We have corn, we have apples, bending down the branches with their weight, and grapes swelling on the vines. There are sweet-smelling herbs and vegetables which can be cooked and softened over the fire, nor are you denied milk or thyme-scented honey. The earth affords a lavish supply of riches, of innocent foods, and offers you banquets that involve no bloodshed or slaughter.

In medieval times vegetarianism was associated with religion as part of the pattern of fast and feast days. The prominent idea was negative – avoidance of meat; there was no evidence of vegetarian food having its own positive attributes. The eighteenth century saw the birth of modern vegetarianism, connected with the first Romantic movement. This ran counter to the dominant ideology which viewed red meat as symbolic of virility, freedom and strength; it was popularly regarded as the very basis

39

of English liberty, fuelling the pioneering exploits of the 'Workhouse of the World' and Empire. Hence the image of John Bull tucking into his roast beef.

Conversely, meat was not seen as wholly appropriate for the weaker sections of society – children, the sick and those in the learning and sedentary occupations. Health manuals of the late nineteenth century suggested a reduction in red meat for pregnant and lactating women, and a diet of fish, chicken or eggs 'that both mirrored the women's own delicate, feminine condition, and avoided stimulation of those qualities of redbloodedness that seemed inappropriate to those fulfilling the nurturing role'.[1]

In the 1930s, vegetarianism became associated with the pacifist and socialist movement, and in the 1960s with hippydom and the tide of protest against the Vietnam war. This explains why, until recently, vegetarianism was often associated as anti-establishment or freakish. Today, however, avoidance of meat is no longer ridiculed. Six per cent of the population are now vegetarian, of which the biggest segments are students and young women. There is also a new but growing phenomenon – the 'demi-veg' people who exist largely on a vegetarian diet, without totally relinquishing meat.

There are various factors which have determined the spread of vegetarianism. Moral or religious conviction against the slaughter of animals is a prime influence; Jains are strictly vegetarian, as are many Buddhists and all but the lowest castes of orthodox Hindus. Vegetarianism also makes sense from a global socio-economic point of view. The raising of livestock in pasture is an extremely inefficient system, as a great deal more food would be yielded from cereal, fruit or vegetable crops grown on an equivalent area of land. Equally, intensively reared animals are fed grains that could otherwise be directed to the poor and undernourished of the world.[2]

Some of the techniques involved in intensive rearing have contributed to the fall in meat consumption. There is widespread disaffection with the confined conditions in which animals are often housed and transported, as well as with the practice of injecting cattle with growth hormones, antibiotics and tranquillisers. A causal connection exists between the incidence of bacterial contamination in meat and poultry and the environments from which they originate. When we learn, from animal welfare groups, of chickens being reared in poorly-ventilated barns, with insufficient room to walk, let alone fly, standing in accumulated faecal matter, it comes as no surprise to discover that, in a survey of North London stores, 80 per cent of frozen chickens were infected with salmonella.[3]

A further important development has been the changing image of vegetarian food. Twenty years ago, pursuit of a non-meat diet invariably involved labouring through a gastronomic wasteland. Today, the scenario has been totally transformed. A virtual cascade of vegetarian cookery books flows forth from the printing presses, brim-full with innovative and imaginative ideas. The technique and finesse of the classical tradition, the introduction of 'new' ingredients from Asia and the Orient, and the lightness and presentation of nouvelle cuisine, have all contributed to a far more exciting meal experience.

Vegetarians are widely perceived as enjoying a 'healthy' diet, and on the whole this would appear to be true as they tend to weigh less and have lower blood pressure than meat eaters. A study of 10 000 volunteers in Britain found a significant negative association between vegetarianism and mortality from coronary heart disease, and similar results have emanated from research in the United States.[4] The equation of vegetarianism with health represents a reversal of former beliefs. Prior to 1750, most medical writers believed fruit and vegetables to have 'evil, pernicious qualities', which caused fevers and 'grievous flux'. This attitude began to change, first when the virtue of fruit rich in vitamin C was appreciated on long sea voyages, and later in the 1930s, when the new science of nutrition discovered the value of minerals, vitamins and fibre. During the Second World War, rationing was organised to increase consumption of foods rich in these nutrients, and recipes were produced to utilise the 'Hedgerow Harvest' of berries, nuts and mushrooms. As a result intake of calcium, iron, vitamin C and many of the B vitamins all rose considerably.

Recent research has shown the vegetarian diet to be perfectly sufficient in protein intake, in terms both of quality and quantity. A little care just needs to be taken to ensure a reasonable balance of sources of protein. For example, pulses tend to be low in the amino-acids methionine and cystine, but rich in lysine, whilst corn is low in lysine but has sufficient methionine and cystine to complement pulses.

There is the possibility of deficiency in certain nutrients, but this can easily be guarded against in the following ways:

1. *Iron* from plant foods is not so well absorbed as that of animal origin, but absorption is much improved if the iron is combined with vitamin C (see examples of this in the recipe section of this book).
2. During the winter months it may be necessary to give *Vitamin D* supplements to vegetarian children and the elderly. Lack of vitamin D hinders calcium absorption, which can lead to rickets in the young and osteomalacia in the old. Some vegetarian Asian women are also at risk if they do not go out a lot (the sun is a source of vitamin D) and do not eat margarine (which contains vitamin D supplement).
3. As fruit and vegetables tend to be bulky but low in calories, the diet must include some high-calorie foods to provide enough *energy* for growth and repair. This is especially important for young children.

A diet overly dependent on high-fat dairy food will inevitably produce an unfavourable nutritional profile. Therefore use of dairy items should be modified in conjunction with the guidelines suggested in Chapter 2. *Vegans* will not encounter this problem as they avoid all dairy products, using soya bean derivatives such as miso, tofu and soya milk. Vegans may become deficient in vitamin B_{12}, as the only sources available to them are bean sprouts, seaweed products, the herb comfrey and fermented drinks such as wine and beer. To guard against inadequate intake, brewer's yeast or B_{12} tablets should be taken as dietary supplements.

If 'demi-veg' people represent a tentative approach to vegetarianism, then Vegans can be seen as the most committed exponents. They avoid all foods that might in any way involve the exploitation of animals, even refusing honey, in the belief, shared by Leonardo da Vinci, that it belongs to the bees alone. Many caterers are happy to create appetising vegetarian dishes, but the absence of dairy products leaves them at a loss when it comes to supplying Vegans. Several of the recipes in this book, such as 'Vegetable Ramekins in Plum Sauce' (p. 90) are appropriate for Vegans, whilst others can easily be adapted by, for instance, omitting yoghurt from some of the soups or replacing gelatine with agar-agar.

Nouvelle cuisine

The phrase 'nouvelle cuisine' is often bandied around without any real understanding of its meaning, and consequently it is popularly misconceived as involving tiny portions of food offered at exorbitant prices. This section will try to provide a constructive explanation of nouvelle cuisine, before considering its value from a nutritional point of view.

'Nouvelle cuisine' was a term coined by Henri Gault and Christian Millau in the October 1973 issue of their gastronomic magazine. It describes the sort cooking being done by the followers of Fernand Point, the famous chef of 'La Pyramide' at Vienne. Point emphasised the importance of fresh produce, and endeavoured to bring out the intrinsic natural flavour of food. He was also a great teacher who tried to break down the tradition of secrecy among chefs, encouraging them to share their knowledge freely. His pupils, such as the celebrated chef-patrons Paul Bocuse, Raymond Thuilier, Françqis Bise, Louis Outhier and the Troisgros brothers, have in turn encouraged and inspired a whole generation of chefs, with their new, lighter style of cookery.

> They threw out the old flour-thickened sauces which occasionally masked the taste, and replaced them with airy concoctions based on reductions of cooking juices. To avoid disguising the ingredients, which were always fresh and of the highest quality, they always placed these sauces *under*, never over the food.[5]

Heavy hors d'œuvres, such as those dense slices of pâté wrapped in solid pastry, gave way to delicate fish mousses, salades composées and light soups. Dishes were designed to excite and stimulate the appetite rather than exhaust it. Feuilletés of pastry were made light as feathers. Hitherto, chefs throughout Europe felt obliged to adhere to the strictures of classical cuisine. A dish eaten in Paris, Vienna or London would be served with the same traditional garnish. By contrast, the exponents of nouvelle cuisine experimented with new combinations of flavours and artistic forms of presentation; chefs everywhere made pictures on plates.

It would be wrong, though, to think that nouvelle cuisine chefs reject the classical tradition. All the leading figures – Point, Bocuse, Guérard – insist on the importance of acquiring a command of the traditional skills, which provides the platform from which to develop one's own creative style. Even when Mosimann was being offered top posts in some of the best known houses in Europe, he decided to spend six months as commis to a master pâtissier, in order to complete the scope of his technical expertise.

Although nouvelle cuisine is regarded as a relatively recent concept, Guérard believes that it in fact relates to a form of creative cookery that can be traced back to the end of the seventeenth century. This 'living French cuisine' historically appears as a resurgent cycle of activity, where chefs propel their craft forward to further levels of achievement. So modern 'nouvelle cuisine' was not a totally new departure, but a movement which shook French cuisine out of a period of relative inertia, reflecting the slogan of May 1968, 'L'imagination prend pouvoir' – all power to the imagination. Escoffier in fact predicted the shape of things to come when he wrote that dishes would become lighter, tastier and more nutritious, with simplicity of presentation being taken 'to its ultimate limits'.[6]

Today there is much talk about nouvelle cuisine having been overtaken by the re-emergence of 'provincial' cooking, with chefs employing the local produce and traditional recipes of a particular region. In reality, though, there is no incompatability between the two styles: a 'nouvelle' approach simply allows a fresh interpretation of long-standing 'provincial' dishes. Perhaps it is inevitable that fashion-conscious food writers will always be keen to announce the arrival of a new style and the demise of an old one. However the influence of modern nouvelle cuisine has been too profound for it to be written off as a passing fad. Raymond Blanc, celebrated chef of 'Le Manoir aux Quatr' Saisons', encapsulates the impact and lasting virtues of nouvelle cuisine, to good effect:

> It is like any revolution, you make mistakes but something of the core is good. Once the excesses have passed, the blood has been spilt, the paranoia has gone, you come back to the truth . . . The best of Nouvelle Cuisine is the beauty and purity of ingredients, their perfect freshness and their transformation within a certain spirit and understanding, stressing lightness, texture, taste and harmony. If that is what someone has in mind, I don't mind being associated with the label. (*A la Carte*, March 1988, p. 62)

There is no automatic link between this type of cooking and healthy eating, as the many 'nouvelle' recipes loaded with cream, butter, sugar and red meats will testify. However, in an age when diet-related disease is strongly connected with over-indulgence, the light, moderately-sized portions of nouvelle cuisine are ideally suited to contemporary levels of energy expenditure. Also the emphasis on fresh produce ensures that the food used is in prime condition, both in terms of natural flavour and of nutritional content.

Some eminent 'nouvelle' chefs have devised specifically healthy forms of cooking, none more significant than Michel Guérard's 'cuisine minceur'. Conceived in 1972, it pre-dated the current vogue for healthfoods and was therefore well ahead of its time. Hitherto, Guérard had attracted attention with his sensationally flavoursome 'gourmand' dishes at 'Le Pot au Feu', a little restaurant on the outskirts of Paris, but following a visit to a health spa he was struck by the image of patients sadly munching their way through platefuls of grated carrot, and resolved to develop a cuisine that was both appetising and nutritious. His declared intentions for 'cuisine minceur' read as pure poetry.

> I wanted to produce a complete festival of light meals for slimming, with salads as fresh as children's laughter, gleaming fish, the heavy scent of forbidden peaches, and roast chicken as deliciously perfumed as those of my childhood picnics.[7]

Being primarily designed for slimmers, 'cuisine minceur' contained very little fat or oil and no sugar. It pioneered many of the adaptations of cooking methods (outlined in Chapter 2) that are necessary for healthy eating, such as dry-sautéing and thickening with vegetable purées. Ever since Guérard began to offer a 'cuisine minceur' menu, his restaurant-cum-health resort at Eugénie-les-Bains has consistently been awarded the highest culinary accolade of three Michelin stars. Perhaps more than any other chef, he has demonstrated the possibility of creating a healthy form of cuisine that is also a joy to eat.

A decade later, Anton Mosimann drew on many of the principles of 'cuisine minceur' to develop his own 'cuisine naturelle'. In the intervening period, the importance of dietary fibre had become more apparent, and this is reflected in Mosimann's recipes. He ignores sugar substitutes, preferring to stick to natural ingredients, and uses only minimal amounts of salt, depending instead on lemon juice, herbs, spices and marinades to provide additional flavour. The influence of a year spent in Japan is clearly reflected in the ingredients, cooking methods and visual splendour of 'cuisine naturelle'. As with Guérard, Mosimann's form of healthy eating has attracted widespread critical acclaim, and he sees it as being ideally suited to today's increasingly health-conscious and fitness-oriented clientele.

Unfortunately access to the gastronomic delight of these master chefs is confined to the very affluent minority, but there is no reason why the principles of their cooking cannot be applied to every level of catering. Michel Guérard has, in fact, attempted to extend the benefits of 'cuisine minceur' as far as possible. Firstly he has developed with Chambourcy a range of chilled dishes for sale in supermarkets. Secondly, he has met the

French Minister of Health, to discuss the possibility of incorporating 'cuisine minceur' in hospital catering. And thirdly, he is involved in setting up a National School of Cooking Arts, at Aire-sur-l'Adour, which will promote both healthy eating and the cult of regional cookery.

Notes and References

1. Twigg, 'Vegetarianism and the meanings of meat', Chapter 2, in A. Murcott, *The sociology of food and eating*, Gower, 1985.
2. C. Spencer, 'Twixt animal and vegetable', *Guardian*, 1 Oct. 1988, p. 27.
3. R. Sprenger, *Hygiene for management*, Highfield, 1985, p. 29.
4. H. Blackholly, *Fruits and vegetables: implications for CHD*, Bradford University Food policy Research Unit, 1987, p. 25.
5. P. Levy, *Observer Weekend Review*, 9 June 1985, p. 1.
6. A. Escoffier, *The Complete Guide of Modern Cookery*, Foreword to 2nd edn.
7. M. Guérard, *Cuisine Minceur*, Pan, 1978, p. 11.

6 Catering for Specialist Diets

Within the context of the new nutritional consensus, certain groups of people have specific dietary requirements. This chapter examines how best to cater for elderly people, diabetics, and those on a gluten-free diet.

Perhaps the most important contribution of the NACNE and COMA Reports is that, for the first time, agreement exists on what constitutes a healthy diet for the population as a whole. Small variations might be needed for certain groups of the population, but generally these can easily be accommodated within the framework of the diet outlined in Chapter 1. For example, the micronutrients particularly important for growing children – calcium and vitamins A, C and D – can simply be provided by fresh fruit and vegetables, oily fish and low-fat dairy produce. No special diet need be contemplated.

Equally, the NACNE and COMA guidelines are totally appropriate in the prevention and treatment of a range of medical conditions, principally coronary heart disease and cancers of the digestive tract. Having said this, certain ailments, and the phenomenon of an ageing population, demand more specific dietary attention. This chapter addresses the particular requirements of catering for elderly people, diabetics and those on a gluten-free diet. Those suffering from other conditions, such as multiple sclerosis and arthritis, are not dealt with here, as agreement has yet to emerge on what constitutes their optimum diet.

The New Diabetic Diet

Diabetes results from a lack of effective insulin, which is the major control agent for maintaining normal blood glucose levels. The milder form of the illness, which develops in middle age, can be treated by diet alone or a combination of diet and pills. The more severe condition, juvenile-onset diabetes, requires treatment by insulin injection, along with adherence to a strict dietary regime.

Most insulin-dependent diabetics are prescribed 24-hour doses, which are administered half an hour before breakfast. The purpose of the medication is to provide peak insulin activity when most carbohydrate is being absorbed by the body. Pulses of insulin are released to coincide with a pattern of mealtimes previously agreed between doctor and patient. It is important that the diabetic sticks closely to this meal programme, otherwise there is the risk either of blood sugar levels soaring unacceptably high, if food is taken when insuffient insulin is available; or of low blood sugar reactions occurring where food consumption does not cover times of peak insulin activity.

Clearly diet is intimately connected with both the nature and the control of the disease. Until very recently, carbohydrate was regarded as the villain of the piece. The rationale behind this thinking went as follows:

All carbohydrates are converted through digestion to glucose and transported to the blood.

Diabetics have problems regulating the level of blood glucose.

Therefore diabetics should seek to minimise the amount of carbohydrate they consume.

Consequently, in 1983, the diabetic diet at the London Hospital recommended that 68 per cent of energy come from fat, 17 per cent from protein and just 15 per cent from carbohydrate. This might seem a rather extreme example, but, overall, conventional medical opinion sought to limit carbohydrate intake to between 30 and 40 per cent of total calories.[1]

Some researchers began to doubt the wisdom of this approach. It was noted that in Asian and African countries, by dint of economic necessity, diabetics consumed diets containing 70–80 per cent carbohydrate, without ill effect. In Britain, Dr Hugh Trowell recorded how, between 1941 and 1954, the number of diabetic deaths fell by half, and this fall coincided with the compulsory use of high-fibre National Flour. It was left to doctors in the United States to incorporate the essence of these findings into a new diabetic regime. In 1976, Kiehm achieved improved control and less need for insulin when patients were transferred to a 75 per cent carbohydrate, high-fibre diet. Comparable results were achieved by Dr James Anderson in Lexington, Kentucky.[2]

This new perspective is based upon an appreciation of the various components of carbohydrate foods: sugars, starches and fibre. When *sugars* are digested on their own by diabetics it is difficult for them to cope with the sudden increase in blood sugar. *Starches*, on the other hand, release their energy more slowly than sugars, and *fibre* in foods slows the absorption even further. So a diet which is high in fibre and starchy foods provides the best chance of achieving good diabetic control.

It is now possible to take an overview of the New Diabetic Diet:

1. *Carbohydrate*   50–60 per cent of energy intake should be in the form of unrefined carbohydrates. The 'gummy' fibres – oats, beans and pulses – are most effective in slowing down the passage of food from stomach to digestive tract. They appear to have a favourable effect on both blood sugar and blood fat levels.

    Since, by definition, diabetes involves a limited tolerance for handling glucose, a balance of moderately-sized meals interspersed with small snacks, should be established. For diabetics dependent on insulin injections, mealtimes should be regulated to meet the timing and intensity of insulin action.

    Sugar should only be consumed during hypoglycaemic (low blood sugar) emergency, or prior to strenuous exercise. Otherwise, total abstention should be observed. The sugar substitutes sorbitol and fructose are of little benefit as they contain about as much energy and refined carbohydrate as their conventional counterparts. In contrast, saccharine and Candarel are acceptable to the British Diabetic Association, as they are substantially lower in energy content.[3]

2. *Fats*   In maturity-onset diabetes, obesity and overweight are common predisposing factors, and in juvenile-onset diabetes they actually inhibit the effectiveness of injected insulin. Fats are the most calorie-packed of all food, and to achieve an optimum body weight diabetics need to reduce fat intake to 30–35 per cent of total calories. Current nutritional thinking associates the high-fat content of the former 'traditional' diabetic diet with coronary heart disease, and a diabetic mortality rate two and a half times the average.[4]

3. Liver and brewer's yeast are rich in something known as *glucose tolerance factor*, of which the mineral chromium is an ingredient. Wholegrains are likewise rich in chromium.

4. *Alcohol* is high in calories, and reduces the body's defence against low blood sugar. For diabetics, alcohol may cause nausea, coma or extreme illness. It should be drunk in moderation – a pint of beer or a glass of wine each day – and never on an empty stomach.

It becomes apparent that the New Diabetic Diet incorporates many of recommendations of the NACNE and COMA Reports. Consequently, most of the recipes in this book will be suitable for diabetics, as they contain predominantly unrefined carbohydrate, no added sugar and are low in fat. The only adjustment necessary would be to reduce the amount of honey used in some of the desserts, or to substitute artificial sweetening or puréed dried fruit.

The Gluten-free Diet

Gluten-free diets are prescribed primarily for treatment of coeliac disease, but also, less commonly, in cases of dermatitis herpetiformis. In coeliac disease, the mucosa and villi in the intestine, responsible for absorption of nutrients, are damaged by gluten. Consequently all sources of gluten have to be avoided: wheat, barley, rye and possibly oats. Until such time as the role of oats is fully understood, it would be wise to omit them. Cereals containing gluten represent a large potential source of fibre, so it is important to ensure that sufficient fibre is obtained from alternative foods such as fruit, vegetables, pulses, rice and nuts.

Clearly, bread, pastry, pasta and breakfast cereals all contain gluten, but in some convenience products its presence is less apparent, and may be disguised by unfamiliar terminology. Avoid foods if the label mentions cereal binder, cereal filler, cereal protein, edible starch, food starch, malt, rusk, rye, vegetable protein and wheat flour. *To be absolutely sure, stick to products carrying the gluten-free symbol*:

There are various gluten-free flours available, such as potato, soya, split-pea, maize, cornflour, rice, sago and buckwheat. The latter has a rather unappealing grey colour, but a distinctive grainy taste. It is used to make the Russian pancakes, blinis, which were traditionally served in *haute cuisine* along with caviar. A recipe for blinis appears in the vegetarian section in Part II. The presence of gluten in any of the other recipes, will be apparent from the list of ingredients.

Catering for Elderly People

Perhaps the most significant demographic change of twentieth-century Britain has been the progressively ageing population. Between 1901 and

1981, the number of pensioners rose from $2\frac{1}{2}$ million to 10 million, and the number of over-80s from 218 000 to $1\frac{1}{2}$ million.

Generally, energy expenditure declines with increasing years, but all too often consumption of food is not reduced accordingly. The NACNE Report estimated that 52 per cent of 60–65-year-olds were overweight, so contributing to the increased incidence of cardio-vascular disease and diabetes.[5] Emphasis should therefore be placed on *quality rather than quantity*, with the provision of moderate-sized portions, attractively presented.

Constipation and dehydration are common problems with the elderly, underlining the importance of adequate dietary fibre and generous fluid intake. Care must also be taken to provide sufficient sources of calcium and potassium. Calcium is less easily absorbed in old age, leading to weakening of the bones. There is evidence that a diet rich in calcium may offset this process of poor absorption, so liberal use should be made of low-fat dairy products, bread, sardines, broccoli, spinach, pulses, nuts and dried fruit. Inadequate intake of potassium has been associated with various ailments, such as muscular weakness, poor grip strength, mental confusion and depression. This can be remedied by regular consumption of skimmed milk, bananas and orange juice.

By the age of 70, half the population no longer have their own teeth, so it would be prudent either to avoid those meat, fruit and salad commodities that cannot easily be chewed, or to select cooking techniques, such as braising and marination, which tenderise food. Taste receptors are also lost with age, owing to atrophy of the taste buds. This can lead to an older person adding excessive quantities of sugar and seasoning in order to register sensations of sweet and salt. Chefs should consider the use of naturally sweet foods, sugar and salt substitutes or alternative flavourings such as lemon, in order to compensate for this taste limitation.

Senior citizens encompass an extremely wide spectrum of people, from those who actively participate in many of the facilities offered by the leisure industry, to those in institutional care. Some will be happy to experiment with innovative dishes, whilst others will be suspicious of 'strange' ingredients, preferring food that is familiar to them. Whichever is the case, the caterer should seek to accommodate the taste preferences of the particular clientele, otherwise attempts to introduce healthy eating onto the menu, may totally backfire.

Notes and References

1. S. Davidson, *et al.*, *Human nutrition and dietetics*, 7th edn, Churchill Livingston, 1979, p. 352.
2. Dr Jim Mann, *The diabetics diet book*, Dunitz, 1985, pp. 9–10. Also, *Policy Statement of the British Diabetic Association*, 'Dietary recommendations for diabetics in the 1980's', BDA, 1983, p. 1.
3. Ibid., BDA statement, p. 7.

4. Davidson, *et al.*, *Human nutrition*, p. 351.
5. The NACNE Report, Health Education Council, 1983, p. 10.

Additional recommended reading
Rawcliff, Peter and Rolph, Ruth, *The gluten-free diet book*, Dunitz, 1985.
Eliopoulos, C., *Geriatric nursing*, Harper & Row, 1979.
Buttriss, J., 'Nutrition and the elderly', *Nutrition and Food Science*, Nov/Dec 1987, p. 10.
Polunin, M., *The New Cookbook*, Macdonald, 1984, pp. 290–5.
Greer, R., *Diets to help multiple sclerosis*, Thorsons, 1982.

7 Nutritional Labelling

> This chapter explains the current legislation relating to nutritional labelling of foods. It also discusses the best ways of expressing the nutritional content of menus.

As recently as the 1960s, there was no requirement for food manufacturers to outline the contents of their products. In Britain, only following a long campaign by *The Sunday Times* did labelling of ingredients become statutory. Today the process has advanced one stage further with the inclusion of nutritional information on food labelling.

Nutritional labelling is beneficial in a number of ways. It facilitates the task of following a healthy diet, helps improve the level of public knowledge and acts as a 'hidden persuader', encouraging manufacturers to reduce fat, sugar and salt contents. Research conducted in 1985 by the Ministry of Agriculture, Food and Fisheries (MAFF) and the National Consumer Council revealed a clear consumer preference for food labels set out in plain and simple terms. Whilst the word 'calories' was widely understood, less than a third of the sample were familiar with either 'kilojoules' or 'kilocalories'. The favourite form of presentation was a bar chart depicting the proportions of energy derived from the principal components of foods.[1]

In the 1980s the British government advanced several proposals for legislation. Perhaps the most impressive Green Paper was that put forward in February 1986, which stipulated a *standard* nutritional format that was to be legally binding on retailers and fast food operators. In the summer of 1987 this proposal was scrapped, partly out of deference to the EC, which might have considered stringent food labelling a barrier to free trade. It has been replaced by the MAFF Proposals for Fat Content of Food Regulations (1987), and the MAFF Guidelines on Nutrition Labelling (1988).

The regulations governing fat require virtually all foods to be labelled with both their total fat and saturated fat content. The main exemptions are fresh fruit and vegetables, bread and cereals: commodities typically low in fat and often sold in unpackaged form.

The guidelines on nutritional labelling are purely *voluntary* in nature, and suggest *four* possible forms of presentation. The first option merely outlines energy, protein, carbohydrate and fat content, and consequently does not even comply with the fat regulation described above, which requires an analysis of saturated fat. The information becomes progressively more comprehensive, until the fourth option provides data on fibre and salt, and breaks down fats into their various fatty acids and carbohydrates into starches and sugars.[2]

These guidelines have attracted a good deal of criticism, principally because of their voluntary basis and also because the four different formats are likely to create more confusion than clarity. Nowhere is there any distinction made between naturally-occurring and added sugars, and vitamins and minerals are omitted altogether. Energy is to be presented in kilojoules or kilocalories, and nutrients are to be listed in gm per 100 gm of food, despite widespread public ignorance of such tabulation. A milk carton labelled as having a fat content of 3.8 gm per 100 gm is meaningless to most people, but if this is expressed as 54 per cent of total energy it immediately indicates a rather high-fat pinta.

It would appear that the opportunity to further nutritional awareness, through establishing a simple, universal system of food labelling, has been wasted. The nutritionist J. T. Winkler encapsulated the shortcomings of the proposed legislation as follows:

> The Guidelines advocate lower standards than current best practice in the food industry. They employ language which MAFF knows people don't understand. And, most absurd, the information will be insufficient for consumers to follow the government's own dietary advice ('If you know what's good for you, don't look at the label', *Guardian*, 4 Sept. 1987, p. 21).

There is greater cause for optimism concerning legislation to control nutritional claims – those banner slogans which seem to adorn almost every food product, announcing that they are either 'low in fat', 'high in fibre' or possessed of wondrous qualities of vitality! In July 1988, the Food Advisory Committee (FAC) recommended legislation which would establish specific criteria for making such claims. In addition, all products emblazoned in this manner would have to provide nutritional labelling containing almost as much detail as the fourth option described above.[3]

Caterers may wish to establish their own system of 'labelling', to highlight healthy dishes on a menu. Some subtlety would be required in more upmarket establishments. People dining out for an expensive meal do not expect to open the menu and be greeted by a diatribe on the evils of fat and sugar. It might be best to offer a selection of dishes under a slightly 'cultivated' heading such as 'Cuisine légère' or 'Cuisine de santé'. At

Michel Guérard's three Michelin star, 'Les Prés d'Eugénie', customers can choose between the standard 'Cuisine Gourmande' menu and the equally delicious, but healthy, 'Cuisine Minceur'. At the 'Ménage à Trôis' in London, Anthony Worrall Thomson has incorporated the demand for smaller portions and lower calories by devising a menu consisting simply of starters and sweets.

In welfare and institutional catering there is a case for being more directive in advocating a healthy choice. The importance of establishing good eating habits at school age cannot be underestimated, and in hospitals healthfoods should be seen as an important component of preventive medicine. Several schools and children's wards use popular cartoon figures to indicate a healthy dish, and some schools operate the traffic light system, with menu items marked red for stop and think, amber for go carefully and green for go ahead.

The public are becoming increasingly aware of what constitutes a healthy diet. Whatever the market, the cardinal rule is to provide *accurate* nutritional information, otherwise all credibility will be lost. Changing cooking practices and purchasing requirements, in line with the recommendations made in chapter 2, should bring a menu within the parameters of NACNE and COMA. If more detailed nutritional information is required, there are several options that can be pursued:

- Lease or buy a nutritional software package, examples of which are available from the British Dietetic Association, Daimler House, Paradise Circus, Queensway, Birmingham B1 2BJ.
- Pay a nutritional consultant to analyse your recipes.
- Cheaper, but more time-consuming, carry out your own analysis, using McCance and Widdowson's *The Composition of Foods* (HMSO, 1978).
- Use recipes from books which provide an appropriate nutritional breakdown of ingredients.

Notes and References

1. V. Wheelock and A. Freckleton, *Nutritional Labelling*, Bradford University Food Policy Research Unit, December 1984, pp. 13–14.
   Anon, 'What consumers want to see . . . ', *Nutrition and Food Science*, September 1985, p. 16.
2. Kirk, T. 'Nutrition Labelling', *Nutrition and Food Science*, May/June 1988, pp. 16–18.
3. T. Kirk, 'New recommendations . . . ', *Nutrition and Food Science*, Sept/Oct 1988, p. 19.

Additional recommended reading
Freckleton, A., *Who is shaping the nutritional label?*, Bradford University Food Policy Research Unit, 1985.
Freckleton, A., *The development of Nutrition Labelling in the UK*, Bradford University, 1988, especially pp. 190–213.
Luba, A., *The food labelling debate*, London Food Commission, 1985.

8 The Vitamin and Mineral Supplement Debate

> Vitamins and minerals are required by the body in
> extremely small quantities – hence the term
> 'micronutrients' – yet they are all essential for health.
> This chapter examines whether the modern trend of
> consuming vitamin and mineral supplements is an
> appropriate one. An outline of the principal sources and
> functions of micronutrients is provided in Appendix IV
> (p. 149).

A survey of almost 2000 adults discovered that the presence of vitamins on
food labelling was the single nutritional factor most likely to encourage
purchase of a food.[1] The perceived health value of vitamins and minerals is
reflected in approximately one in five people buying dietary supplements.
In 1987, this accounted for a £120 m slice of the 'healthfood' market.[2]

Some nutritionists have questioned the wisdom of consuming these
supplements: firstly, several vitamins and minerals cannot easily be stored
in the body, and when taken in large quantities are simply excreted;
secondly, in some cases excessive intake can produce harmful symptoms,
for example:

- too much vitamin A   can lead to drowsiness, headache and skin peeling;
- too much vitamin D   may result in calcium being deposited in the soft tissues;
- too much vitamin E   interferes with the function of vitamin K, so reducing the blood's ability to coagulate;
- too much zinc   can prevent the body absorbing calcium and iron.

Finally, it is contended that a balanced diet should easily provide enough
vitamins and minerals to meet the 'Recommended Daily Amounts'

(RDAs) set by the Department of Health. This would indeed be a conclusive argument, were it not for the fact that RDAs in Britain are just about the lowest in Europe, and large sections of the population in no way consume a balanced diet.

Table 8.1 demonstrates the low RDAs set in Britain as compared with the United States and the Soviet Union. Several vitamins and minerals are not even accredited in this country and there is virtually no attention paid to the special needs of pregnant women. Significantly, the UK standards have remained virtually unchanged since they were conceived in the 1950s, in contrast with the US standards which are based on nutritional knowledge pertaining in the late 1970s.

Table 8.1   Recommended daily amounts for vitamins and minerals

Vitamins	UK Adult	UK Pregnant woman	US Adult	US Pregnant woman	USSR Adult	USSR Pregnant woman
A mcg	750	750	1 000	1 000	1 500	1 750
D mcg	2.5	10	5	10	2.6	12.5
E mg	None	None	10	10	15	17.5
K mcg	None	None	110	110	250	250
C mg	30	60	60	80	80	150
B_1 mg	1.2	1	1.4	1.4	1.8	2.5
B_2 mg	1.6	1.6	1.6	1.6	2.5	3.25
B_3 mg	18	18	18	16	20	20
B_6 mg	None	None	2.2	2.6	2	4
B_{12} mg	2	2	3	4	2	12.5
Folic acid mcg	300	300	400	800	400	400
Panothenic acid mg	None	None	5.5	5.5	10	27.5
Biotin mcg	None	None	150	150	None	None
Minerals						
Potassium mg	None	None	3 750	3 750	3 750	3 750
Sodium mg	None	None	2 200	2 200	5 000	7 500
Chloride mg	None	None	3 400	3 400	5 000	5 000
Calcium mg	500	1 200	800	1 200	800	1 500
Phosphorous mg	None	None	800	1 200	1 600	2 500
Magnesium mg	None	None	350	450	500	925
Iron mg	12	15	10	48	17.5	17.5
Zinc mg	None	None	15	20	12.5	12.5
Copper mg	None	None	2.5	2.5	2.5	2.5
Iodine mcg	140	140	150	150	150	150
Selenium mcg	None	None	125	125	None	None
Chromium mcg	None	None	125	125	None	None

Source: Geoffrey Cannon, 'The lowest standard in Europe', *Independent*, 2 June 1987, p. 13.

Vitamin deficiencies that produced diseases such as pellagra, scurvy and beriberi are now almost unknown in Western society. However, diet-related cases of anaemia, rickets and osteomalacia still persist, primarily amongst the poorest social groups.[3] In addition, there are large sections of the population whose diet is marginally deficient in various micronutrients, and who would benefit from supplements.[4] The main risk groups are:

- People such as the elderly, disabled and mentally ill, who have difficulty preparing their own meals.
- People living in institutions who have little control over what they eat.
- People, especially children and teenagers, whose diets are largely comprised of convenience and takeaway foods which may have lost much nutritional value during refinement and processing.
- People who cannot afford sufficient fresh produce. Table 8.2 reveals how those in the poorer north of the country eat less fresh fruit and vegetables – source of many vitamins and minerals – than those in the more affluent south.

Table 8.2 Fresh produce intake per person per week (gm)

	Fresh green vegetables	Fresh fruit
SW England	442	671
SE England	375	649
N England	294	440
Scotland	196	513

Source: D. Shrimpton 'Diet off balance', *Nutrition and Food Science*, May 1985, p.7.

Those areas of the country with the worst nutritional standards have the highest incidence of babies born with deformities, such as spina bifida. Prescription of multivitamin/mineral tablets have been shown to reduce the recurrence of deformed children being born to high-risk mothers.[5]

Supplements would also be appropriate for people recovering from illness and surgery, who often lack the motivation to eat normal-sized meals. Smokers, alcoholics, people taking the contraceptive pill or prescribed regular aspirin all require additional vitamin C. Although it is commonly supposed that the body cannot utilise more than 100 mg of vitamin C a day, 5 per cent of a sample study absorbed a daily level of 5000 mg. Linus Pauling, Nobel Prizewinner and author of *Vitamin C and the Common Cold* (W. H. Freeman, 1970), takes a daily gram of the vitamin, which is a far cry from the British RDA of 30 mg.[6]

Recent research attributes selenium and vitamins A, C and E with a positive role in preventive medicine. They may be able to neutralise naturally occurring aggressive particles of 'free radicals', which might otherwise spark off coronary heart disease and cancer.[7]

The whole concept of healthy eating belongs very much to a holistic approach to life where the fruits of the earth are produced and prepared with minimal refinement, in order to promote mental and physical well-being. The manufacture of nutritional supplements in capsule form is perhaps a long way removed from this ideal, but if they can help reduce the incidence of disease and deformity then surely they are something to be utilised in a judicious manner.

Notes and References

1. MAFF, *Food Hygiene – a consumer survey*, HMSO, 1988, p. 20.
2. Anon, 'Food Facts', *Nutrition and Food Science*, Jan. 1989, p. 20.
3. J. Buttriss and M. Turner 'Vitamins, minerals and Health', *Fact File 3*, National Dairy Council Nutrition Service, 1988.
4. Anon, 'New Vitamin Information Service', *Nutrition and Food Science*, July/ August 1988, p. 21.
5. H. Wright, 'Swallow it whole', *New Statesman Pub.*, 1983, p. 6.
   C. Walker, 'The case for vitamin supplements', *Independent*, 13 Jan. 1987, p. 15.
6. C. Austen, 'Vitamin C requirements', *Nutrition and Food Science*, March/April 1988, p. 18.
7. C. Walker, The case for vitamin supplements.
   Anon, 'A new vitamin information service', *Nutrition and Food Science*, July/August 1988, p. 21.

Additional Recommended Reading
Bender, A., *Health or hoax*, Elvendon Press, 1985.
Ferriman, A., 'The great minerals gold mine', *Observer*, 22 May 1988, p. 7.
Buttriss, J., 'Vitamins and minerals'; 'Free radicals', *'Nutrition and Food Science'*, Jan/Feb 1989, pp. 7–12.

9 The Importance of Safe and Hygienic Practice for a Healthy Diet

No study of healthy eating can ignore the procedures necessary to ensure the safe and wholesome nature of food served to the public. This chapter summarises the essential elements of hygienic kitchen practice, before extending the scope of discussion to encompass the food production chain as a whole.

Food poisoning outbreaks now represent a major threat to public health in the United Kingdom. In 1987, over 20 000 cases were reported in England and Wales alone, an increase of 100 per cent on the 1982 figure. By 1988 the number of cases had doubled once more, to 41 196.[1] Alarming though these statistics are, they fail to reflect the magnitude of the problem, as notified cases of food poisoning form just a fraction of the true total. Several factors have contributed to the deteriorating situation: the increase in high-protein convenience foods, the proliferation of takeaway snack-food outlets and improper use of certain new food production systems. While it would be wrong to underestimate the size of the problem, it is by no means an insurmountable one. Adherence to a set of simple, common-sense procedures would establish good hygienic practice at every level of the catering industry.

Adherence to Correct Temperature Control

Temperature	Effect on bacteria
	Most bacteria are destroyed
70°C	
	Activity slackens but bacteria survive
45°C	
	Rapid reproduction
15°C	
	Activity slackens
3°C	
	Little or no activity, but some bacteria such as listeria continue to propagate at these temperatures
0°C	
− 18°C	Bacteria survive but remain dormant

59

Thorough cooking at 70°C destroys the vast majority of bacteria, so it is important that all foods, especially meat, are cooked up to this temperature. It is well worth investing in a temperature probe, so that chefs can ascertain the internal temperature of a joint of meat or a carcass of chicken.

Frozen poultry is a notoriously common source of food poisoning, and it is essential to defrost the birds thoroughly prior to cooking. They should be placed on the bottom shelf of a fridge, as birds left to thaw in the open kitchen will warm up on the surface while the inside remains frozen. If poultry is only partially defrosted, the cooking process will merely serve to thaw out and warm the centre of the carcass, so creating an ideal temperature for bacterial growth. The practice of stuffing the cavity should be avoided as this inhibits thorough heat penetration of the carcass. Far safer, and tastier, to stuff poultry under the skin, as in the recipe for 'Parslied Chicken' (p. 106).

If food is not to be served immediately it should be held above 65°C or, alternatively, chilled or frozen for storage. Chilling and freezing should be carried out rapidly to avoid the possibility of recontamination through airborne bacteria. All too often, cooked meats are simply left to 'cool' for hours in the kitchen, which invariably means resting in the ambient, moist environment in which bacteria thrive. The temperature of the food can be swiftly brought down by using an ice bath or blast chiller/freezer. In the absence of such equipment, the food should not be put in an ordinary fridge; this will merely result in the fridge and its contents warming up. Instead, the food should be transferred from the cooking utensil into a clean container, and placed in a sink of flowing cold water. Once cool it should be covered and put in the fridge.

The whole question of chilling foods is very topical, as a result of the growing popularity of 'cook–chill' and 'sous-vide' systems. Current Department of Health regulations recommend that, cook–chilled food should be:

Cooked to an internal temperature of 70°C for at least two minutes	Rapidly chilled to 0–3°C within 90 minutes of cooking	Held at 0–3°C for a maximum of 5 days	Regenerated to 70°C prior to service
→	→	→	

However a study by Environmental Health Officers (EHOs) in 1988 revealed that only 19 per cent of hospitals using cook–chill actually operated within these guidelines.[2] The hygiene implications of temperature abuse are considerable, as several bacteria, such as listeria, yersinia and the E strain of botulinum, have been found to multiply at temperatures previously regarded as safe. Attention has focused particularly upon listeria monocytogenes, which is capable of multiplying at 3°C, and experiences an explosion in growth rate after five days at 7.5°C. Listeriosis food poisoning is particularly dangerous for babies, pregnant women and the elderly, and carries a 30 per cent fatality rate. There has been a strong lobby in the catering press for the Department of Health regulations to be tightened, so that:

- cook–chill and sous-vide systems are only allowed to operate under licence;
- the holding time of chilled foods is limited to just three days.

Avoidance of Cross-contamination

One of the commonest causes of food poisoning is cross-contamination between raw and cooked foods. The easiest way of avoiding this is to establish a logical flow of production in the kitchen:

Delivery → Storing → Food preparation → Cooking → Holding or portioning → Serving

Such a system is easiest to operate in a large kitchen, where there is sufficient space to ensure distinctive storage and preparation areas of meat, fish, poultry and dairy products, and separate provision for cooked and uncooked foods. Unfortunately space is at a premium in most kitchens, and often all food commodities are handled in the same area and held in common fridges. If this is the case several precautions need to be taken:

- use a colour-coding system for chopping boards, so that each board is used only for a specific food commodity;
- carefully clean hands, knives and work surfaces before starting on a fresh food commodity;
- demarcate separate areas of the fridge for different commodities, cover and clearly label all refrigerated items, and place raw meats on the bottom shelf so that there is no possibility of blood dripping onto other foods and contaminating them.

Good Standards of Personal Hygiene

All too often, changing and toilet facilities in catering establishments are cramped, inadequate and irregularly cleaned. Inevitably, such limited provision does nothing to establish good standards of personal hygiene among staff, so employers would be wise to invest in *first-rate facilities*.

Changing rooms should contain a sufficient number of sinks and showers, and be equipped with disposable towels and soap dispensers, rather than the linen towels and bars of soap which act as vehicles for the transfer of bacteria. In the kitchen, wash-hand basins should be provided apart from food preparation and pot wash sinks. All toilet and washing facilities should be cleaned daily, and chefs' whites and cloths should be laundered regularly.

Having established a good standard of amenities, the caterer is in a position to demand the very best of his or her staff in terms of personal hygiene. Hair should be tied back and covered, nails kept clean and short, and rings, bracelets and watches removed to prevent cross-contamination. The popular image of a bad chef includes an ash-laden cigarete hanging perilously, Andy Capp style, over a cooking pot. It goes without saying that all smoking should be banned in the kitchen.

Unfortunately, in an industry typified by long hours, there is a tendency for some staff to soldier on even when they are patently unfit for work. In a kitchen this can result in infection spreading to colleagues and clientele alike. Such staff should be sent home, especially if they are suffering from stomach upsets or skin conditions. Any cuts should be properly bandaged and protected, and care should be taken to use disposable gloves when dealing with open wounds, so as to avoid possible infection from AIDS.

Establishing a Good Cleaning System

Frequently responsibility for cleaning is delegated to the lowest grade in the hierarchy, the kitchen porter, whose work is typically poorly paid and devoid of any meaningful job satisfaction. As a result, staff turnover at this level is usually high and the standard of work suffers accordingly. There are two possible ways round this problem: first, the porter's pay and status could be elevated to that of 'hygiene operative', which would reflect the importance of maintaining a good standard of cleanliness in the kitchen; second, a collective responsibility for hygiene could be established by involving *all* catering staff in a cleaning rota.

There may be obvious pieces of equipment, such as work surfaces, which are routinely cleaned down, but several areas require more careful attention to detail.

- Slicing and mincing machines should be dismantled and cleaned after use, as they are common sources of cross-contamination.
- Fridge interiors require thorough cleaning, as bacteria can multiply at these relatively low temperatures.
- Hot cabinets should be kept free from spillage and encrusted food debris.

- Tin-openers should not be overlooked, as dirt and grime that build up around the cutting edge can drop into food.
- Air extractor filters and the drip trays which hang beneath them should be regularly soaked in hot detergent to prevent the build-up of grease.
- Ideally, food waste should be put through waste disposal units, but if bins are used they should be lined, covered and regularly cleaned.
- All areas of floor and wall space should be accessible, to prevent dirt and debris accumulating in nooks and crannies.

Establish Confidence in the Supplier

A significant proportion of food poisoning outbreaks derive from contamination at the source of supply. Restaurateurs who deal directly with farmers and producers (see Chapter 3) will easily be able to satisfy themselves as to the wholesome standard of food deliveries. However, for most caterers, the origins of supply are much more remote, and the safe and hygienic quality of goods can only be accepted on trust. In recent years a series of incidents have combined to damage public trust and confidence in certain aspects of the food-chain. Two of these incidents are examined here in order to appreciate the extent of the problem, and the possible ways in which standards of safety can be improved.

The Outbreak of Salmonella Enteritidis in Eggs

Poultry is a notorious source of contamination, accounting for half the number of food poisoning cases each year.[3] In the 1970s, entire flocks of hens were laid low by salmonella pullorum, and more recently it has been estimated that 80 per cent of frozen chickens are contaminated with various strains of salmonella.[4] The outbreak of salmonella enteritidis phage type 4 is especially worrying, as the bacteria actually enter into the egg itself, but do not interfere with the egg-laying process. This means that infected eggs continue to be produced without any visible sign of disease in the hen.

The number of food poisoning cases related to salmonella enteritidis more than doubled during 1988.[5] As a result, the goverment's chief medical officer advised caterers to avoid all egg recipes which do not achieve pasteurisation temperature. These include mayonnaise, hollandaise, sabayon and their derivatives; omelettes, poached and soft-boiled eggs; meringue, ice cream and custards. A whole segment of the chef's repertoire could no longer be guaranteed as safe.

The increased incidence of chronic infection in poultry has been directly attributed to intensive methods of production.[6] Five battery hens are contained within a cage measuring 45×50 cm ($18'' \times 20''$), and up to 30 000 live in one unit. Two million hens die in their cages each year as a result of exhaustion and overcrowding. In such conditions of close confinement disease can only flourish. The birds exist on a diet of animal protein feeds, 10–30 per cent of which is itself infected with salmonella.[7] The 1981 Protein Processing Order, ostensibly designed to eradicate contamination in feeds, in fact permits the inclusion of:

> any part of any dead animal or bird, or of any fish, reptile, crustacean, blood, hatchery waste, eggs, hair, horns, hide, hoofs, feather and *any material which contains human effluent*.[8]

There is nothing inevitable about the unpalatable features associated with this method of raising poultry. The legislative powers exist under Section 8 of the 1984 Food Act to prosecute unhygienic poultry companies. Additionally, scientific research has developed several means of reducing the incidence of disease:

- Treatment of protein feeds with organic acids can lower the rate of infection to less than 1 per cent.[9]
- Glasgow University veterinary school has found a way of detecting the microscopic flaws in eggs which make them vulnerable to infection.[10]
- The British Institute of Food Research developed a natural means of 'crowding out' salmonella, by encouraging the growth of harmless micro-organisms in the hen's gut. Unfortunately the project had its funding withdrawn just 12 months from fruition.

These research projects deserve to receive adequate government funding. Equally, MAFF could incorporate egg and poultry farming into the scheme of incentives, now being developed, to de-intensify agriculture. Colin Spencer has suggested that, if just one in four farms kept a flock of 1000 free-range hens, then current demand for eggs could still be satisfied.

The Outbreak of BSE in Cattle

In 1981, permission was granted for the offal and brains of sheep to be included in concentrated grain feed for cattle. Sheep have long suffered from a viral brain disease known as scrapie, and by 1986 it became apparent that scrapie-infected feed had transmitted the disease to cattle in the form of bovine spongiform encephalopathy (BSE). Over the next two years, 2180 cases of BSE were reported, afflicted animals suffering acute distress and ultimately having to be put down.[11]

The disease may similarly be transmitted to other mammals: in humans it manifests itself in the brain disorders Kuru and Creutzfeldt-Jacob dementia. Beef offal, including brains, are components of various meat products, and it is quite possible that the brains of infected animals have already entered the food-chain in the form of pies, pâtés, tinned meat and consommé.

The virus survives all normal methods of sterilisation and, consequently, Dr Helen Grant, senior consultant in brain diseases at Charing Cross Hospital, believes that all beef offal should be incinerated, until such time as BSE has been totally wiped out.[12] The scientific working party set up under Sir Richard Southwood to investigate the problem questioned the 'unnatural feeding practices' whereby ruminant meat is fed to other ruminants. Certainly the serious health risk posed by this example of intensive animal husbandry reinforces the case for traditional farming practices, such as simply feeding cattle on grass and hay. If concentrated protein feeds must be used, soya-based products offer a greater degree of safety.

The government is making a number of positive moves in terms of improving the hygienic quality of food served to the customer. They are seriously considering *compulsory* hygiene training for catering establishments and, through the 'Heartbeat' scheme, are rewarding caterers who provide healthy eating choices from kitchens that are hygienically up to standard. It would be equally encouraging if a similar combination of scrutiny and incentive was directed at the supply end of the food chain. *If the fundamental nutritional contribution of the 1980s was to define the shape of a healthy diet, perhaps the principal task facing the 1990s will be to ensure the safe and wholesome nature of the food supply.*

Notes and References

1. Editorial, *Nutrition and Food Science*, July/August 1988.
   C. Hall 'Food poisoning . . . ', *Independent*, 23 Mar. 1989, p. 7.
   MAFF Consumer Survey, *Food Hygiene*, HMSO, 1988, p. 5.
2. Anon, 'Listeria Hysteria', *Caterer and Hotelkeeper*, 19 Jan. 1989, p. 6.
3. Anon, 'Salmonella . . . ', *Nutrition and Food Science*, March 1989, p. 10.
4. R. Sprenger, *Hygiene for management*, Highfield, 1985, p. 29.
5. Anon, *The Food Magazine*, Spring 1989, p. 2.
6. C. Spencer, 'Fatal assault on the batteries', *Guardian Weekend*, re Fifth symposium of the British Vetinerary Association, 17 Dec. 1988.
7. R. North 'Ministry to blame . . . ', *Independent*, 19 Dec. 1988, p. 3.
8. C. Spencer, 'Truth has flown the coop . . . *Guardian Weekend*, 4 Mar. 1989, p. 15.
9. O. Gillie, 'Incubation of an epidemic', *Independent*, 20 Dec. 1988, p. 15.
10. G. Webb, 'Egg study funds . . . ', *Caterer and Hotelkeeper*, 23 Feb. 1989, p. 9.
11. R. North, 'Concentrated feed linked . . . *Independent*, 28 Feb. 1989, p. 2.
12. Anon, *The Food Magazine*, Summer 1989, p. 3.

Part II
The Recipes

Introduction

These recipes reflect a variety of influences: the honest authenticity of provincial cooking, the lightness and imagination of nouvelle cuisine, and the wealth of 'new' ingredients – once considered exotic but now so readily available – which provide an extra dimension of flavour. Approximately half the dishes have been developed by the author, but the remainder have more illustrious origins. There are three derived from Michel Guérard and Jane Grigson, and two from Miriam Polunin and Leslie Forbes.

No attempt has been made to replicate those rather clichéd examples of 'healthy' menus, such as nutloaf, quiche or lentil bake. Equally, little space has been devoted to modifications of traditional dishes, such as a leaner Shepherd's Pie; these can easily be achieved by following the suggestions outlined in Chapter 2. Instead, the intention is to provide a repertoire of novel and appetising dishes which stimulate the tastebuds, and reveal healthy eating as an *enjoyable* meal experience.

Nutritional Profile

All the recipes have been nutritionally analysed by Wendy Doyle (SRD) at the Nuffield Laboratory of Contemporary Medicine, London. This enables a comparison to be made with the principal recommendations of the NACNE and COMA Reports. To recap briefly, these state that:

- total energy intake should equal total energy expenditure. For the average adult this means a daily requirement of 2000–2500 kilocalories.
- overall fat consumption should represent no more than 30–35 per cent of energy intake.
- saturated fat consumption should represent no more than 10–15 per cent of energy intake.
- consumption of fibre should increase by 50 per cent to 30 gm daily.
- consumption of refined sugar should fall by half to 50 gm daily.
- consumption of salt should fall by 25 per cent to 9 gm daily.

Each recipe is accompanied by nutritional information on energy, total fat, saturated fat and fibre. *None of the recipes contains any added sugar*, all sweetening coming from fruit and small amounts of honey. As for salt, up to 70 per cent of average intake derives from processed foods, virtually all of which have been excluded here. This being the case, it should be quite permissible to lightly season the dishes with salt.

It would be extremely difficult to devise a menu in which every recipe conformed precisely to NACNE and COMA criteria. *The important thing is to achieve an optimum nutritional balance over a whole day's eating.* A few of the recipes that follow derive more than 35 per cent of their energy from fat, but they also contain important nutrients, such as the essential fatty acids in oily fish and a wealth of vitamins and minerals in liver. Clearly it would be counterproductive to exclude these dishes through adherence to a rigid nutritional formula. Overall, the recipes in this book can be used confidently as part of a genuinely healthy diet.

Quantities

All the savoury dishes have been designed for 4–6 covers; there are just a few desserts which cannot practically be made in such small quantities. No problems should be encountered when scaling up production. Higher National Diploma students have successfully prepared many of the recipes for 20 covers, and quantities of 60 or more have been provided for lunches at 'La Maison Française' in Oxford.

Recipe ingredients are all given in metric terms, so the following table should prove helpful for those more conversant with imperial tabulation.

Imperial unit	Metric equivalent (approx.)
1 oz	28 gm
4 oz	112 gm
8 oz	225 gm
1 lb	450 gm
2 lb	900 gm
2.2 lb	1 kilo
$\frac{1}{4}$ pint	140 ml
$\frac{1}{2}$ pint	280 ml
1 pint	570 ml
1.8 pint	1 litre

Glossary of Terms

Recipe methods are described using terminology well established in working kitchens and catering colleges. However, if any are unfamiliar, an explanation is provided below.

Al dente   Vegetables cooked so that they retain a little crispness and crunchiness.

Bain-marie   A 'water bath' used to achieve gentle heat penetration of food: for example, eggs whisked in a bowl that rests above a pan of steaming water. This facilitates maximum aeration, without coagulation of the eggs. Alternatively, food baked in the oven, in a container which is half-immersed in a tray of hot water.

Baking blind   The method of baking crisp pastry cases in a moderate oven. The flan ring or tartlet dish is light oiled, closely lined with pastry, and left to rest in the fridge for half an hour. The base is then pricked with a fork to prevent rising or bubbling during cooking. The flan ring needs to be lined with greaseproof paper and filled with dried beans, to stop the sides from collapsing; this is not absolutely necessary with small tartlet moulds, as they retain their shape quite well during cooking. Once the pastry case has 'set' (10–20 minutes depending on the size), it can be removed from the mould, and returned to the oven without the baking beans. This final stage further enhances the crispness of the product. Although wholemeal pastry is obviously brown in colour, it does darken discernibly when fully cooked.

Batons   The term used to describe vegetables cut into thin rectangles – approximately 5 cm ($2\frac{1}{2}''$ long) – and used for crudités, garnishes and salads. An equivalent French term is 'jardinière'.

Blanching   The brief immersion of vegetables in boiling liquid, to soften or part-cook them.

Brunoise   A very fine dice of vegetables. To achieve an onion brunoise, peel the onion and cut in half, bisecting the root. Slice each onion half very thinly, cutting towards the root but not through it. Then slice across, again very thinly. Discard the root stump, and chop the onion together finely, using a large-bladed knife.

Concasser   This is a term used for a technique involving the skinning of tomatoes. With a vegetable knife, cut a small incision in that green/yellow part of the tomato which originally attached the fruit to the plant. Plunge the tomato into rapidly boiling water for 10–20 seconds (depending on the degree of ripeness), immerse in cold running water and drain. Cut around the circumference, and the skin should peel away quite easily. Classically, an uncooked concasse involves quartering the tomato and removing the pips, but this obviously reduces the nutritional content. A cooked concasse is the tomato pulp, gently sweated down with a fine dice of onion and garlic.

Coulis   A sauce, generally made from soft fruit, which is liquidised and poured onto a plate. This provides the 'canvas' on which to place the main food item. The coulis can be decorated with thin lines or twirls of yoghurt. Straining a coulis provides an impressive sheen, but reduces the fibre content.

Deglaze   When meat or fish is cooked in a sauteuse or roasting tray, a flavoursome, caramelised sediment is left stuck to the bottom of the pan. This can be incorporated into a sauce by removing the main food item, placing the pan on the stove, and swilling round with stock or alcohol while scraping vigorously with a wooden spoon. Deglazing over a high heat drives off most of the calories in alcohol, while intensifying the flavour of the cooking liquor.

Dégraisser   To skim off the fat from a stock, sauce or soup. If the liquid is rapidly chilled and refrigerated overnight, the fat will congeal on the surface, and can easily be removed the following morning.

Glaze   A stock that is reduced down to a thick, barely moving consistency. This then forms the basis for a sauce.

Julienne   A very delicate cut of vegetables used frequently as a garnish. The vegetable is squared off, cut into thin slices about 4 cm ($1\frac{1}{2}''$) long, and then each sliver is cut into fine shreds.

Mandolin   A manually operated piece of equipment used to achieve consistently thin slices of vegetables. It also possesses a corrugated blade for cutting 'gaufrette' potatoes.

Picking   Applied to parsley or spinach, this means to remove the stalks.

Proving   The resting of yeast dough in a warm moist environment. This provides the ideal conditions for yeast to work effectively. Generally a dough is left to prove, and then 'knocked back': kneaded vigorously for 3–4 minutes. It is then formed into the desired shape, and left to prove again before baking.

Prove a crêpe pan   Rub with sea salt and steep in oil overnight. Bring to just short of smoking temperature and pour out the oil. Then cool, wipe clean and dry with kitchen paper. The pan will now retain its non-stick quality, so long as it is not washed with detergent and hot water. Proving in this way, allows crêpes to be made without adding any oil to the pan.

Refresh   To plunge cooked vegetables into cold, flowing water, in order to arrest the cooking process and thereby retain colour and crispness. Once cold, the food is drained and held ready for service.

Stock   A flavoured liquid used for soups, sauces, stews, and braised dishes. A genuine stock provides the foundation for all good cuisine. Vegetable stocks are the most simple to make; an appropriate selection of vegetables and herbs are simmered for 40–50 minutes, and then strained. For fish stocks, the scored fish bones are gently sweated down for a few minutes with lemon juice and a dice of onion. The ingredients are then covered in cold water and brought to a simmer for 25–30 minutes. As with all stocks, the surface should be regularly skimmed to remove fat and impurities. Chicken stock is made by gently simmering chicken carcasses, root vegetables, herbs and parsley stalks for 4–6 hours. Meat stocks are cooked for a few hours longer, using beef or veal bones. For a brown meat stock, the bones should first be roasted in the oven.

Sweating down   This is the process of gently cooking food in a little hot fat for a few minutes, under cover. It is used primarily as a means of softening root vegetables. Many traditional recipes use quite excessive quantities of fat; in fact, the saucepan need only be brushed with a little unsaturated oil.

Soups

The soup pot was an endless centrepiece, providing a nourishment whose anticipatory odours nurtured the appetite . . . The great yiddish writer Peretz has a story told about a magical pot which contained the soup of centuries. Blackened on the hearth, never emptied, in days of prosperity it produced untold riches while in hard times, as plain water was added, it derived the flavour of survival from generations of soup . . . (Keith Botsford, 'Hubble bubble no toil no trouble', *The Independent*, 30 Jan. 1988, p. 14)

In many ways we have lost touch with a variety of common, edible plants which often grow in abundance around us. In medieval times, young nettle leaves were greatly prized, being the first green vegetables to appear after the rigours of winter. Likewise, dandelion, lavender and all manner of herbs were common constituents of the soup pot, *Culpepper's Herbal* according them all miraculous curative properties! The nourishing and wholesome nature of soup in fact provides the origins for the word 'restaurant' – from the French verb 'restaurer': to restore, invigorate – as the early restaurants in France only served soups and broths.

The basis of good soup is a good stock and, if using meat bones or carcasses of poultry and game, make sure the surface is regularly skimmed during cooking. The most effective way of removing fat is to rapidly chill the finished stock, refrigerate overnight, and then lift off the congealed surface layer in the morning. Vegetable stocks contain only negligible amounts of fat, as no sweating of ingredients is required. They take just an hour to prepare, by simply simmering a selection of herbs and vegetables appropriate to the finished dish.

In recent years, vegetarian recipes have greatly influenced soup-making, with their imaginative combinations of fruit and vegetables. Another important development has been the invention of the blender. The ease with which food can be pureed means that soups no longer have to be thickened with roux, egg yolks, butter or cream, and as a result they taste much more distinctly of their principal ingredients.

Butterbean, Carrot and Yoghurt Soup

This is a creamy, warming winter soup. As well as providing protein and fibre, butterbeans are a good sauce of iron and zinc. Carrots are extremely rich in vitamin A, and also contain folic acid and vitamin C.

Ingredients   **5 portions**

15 ml sunflour oil	350 gm carrot
200 gm dried butterbeans	100 gm celery
150 ml skimmed milk	100 gm potato
Seasoning. Nutmeg	80 gm Greek yoghurt
$\frac{1}{4}$ teaspoon of Marmite	80 gm low-fat set yoghurt
150 gm onion	

Nutritional analysis per portion

Energy: 218 KCals
Fibre: 12 g
Fat: 5.3 g

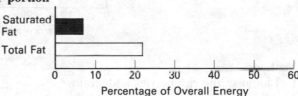

Method

1. Soak the beans overnight.
2. Drain and rinse. Put the beans in a pan, cover with water and bring up to a simmer. Stir in the Marmite, and leave to simmer gently.
3. Peel and finely dice the onions and garlic and sweat down in a little oil. Peel or simply scrub the carrots and potatoes, roughly chop, along with the celery, and add to the gently cooking onions. Continue to sweat down for 2–3 minutes. Add the butterbeans and their cooking liquor, and enough milk to make quite a thick soup. Season, cover and allow to simmer for 40 minutes.
4. Remove from the heat for a few minutes and then stir in the yoghurt. Blend in the food processor. Bring back to the heat and adjust for seasoning.

Raspberry and Orange Soup

A lovely, fresh summer soup, for one of those rare sunny days! Orange juice is rich in vitamin C and potassium, and raspberries, like all berries, are a good source of fibre. To retain all the fibre, do not strain the soup.

Ingredients   **4 portions**
Juice of 2 oranges   50 gm fluid, low-fat yoghurt
750 gm fresh raspberries   1 teaspoon acacia honey

Nutritional analysis per portion
Energy: 67 KCals
Fibre: 14 g
Fat: 0.1 g

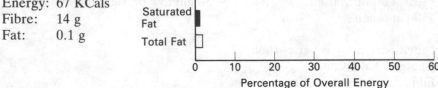

Method
1. Liquidise the raspberries and strain.
2. Add a little honey to taste (acacia honey sweetens without contributing a distinctive honey flavour). Equally, add orange juice to taste.
3. Serve chilled, with a twirl of yoghurt.

Lentil and Apricot Soup

This soup makes use of green lentils, which in the days of the Roman Empire were accorded the highest possible status. 'Each of the four major legumes known to Rome lent its name to a prominent Roman family; Fabius came from the faba bean, Lentulus from the *lentil*, Piso from the pea, and Cicero – most distinguished of them all – from the chick pea. No other food group has been so honoured.' (*Guardian* Food and Drink page, 12 Sept. 1986)

Unlike other dried beans and pulses, lentils do not require a long soaking prior to cooking. They merely require an hour, as this allows the grit and sediment often attached to lentils to be easily rinsed away. The dried apricots can also be roughly chopped and soaked for half an hour. This helps bring out their flavour during the cooking process. So as not to lose any nutrients, the water the apricots have been steeped in can be added to the soup. Dried apricots are exceptionally high in beta-carotene, which is the plant form of vitamin A. Recent research reveals that people with a high level of beta-carotene in their bodies experience a lower incidence of cancer.

Ingredients   5 portions
150 gm green lentils   Seasoning. 6 cardamom pods
100 gm dried apricot   15 ml sunflower oil
120 gm onion   50 gm Greek yoghurt
1 clove of garlic   50 gm low-fat set yoghurt
Sufficient veg. stock or water to
make a thick-consistency soup

Nutritional analysis per portion
Energy: 180 KCals
Fibre: 9 g
Fat: 4.5 g

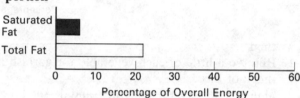

Method
1. Soak the lentils and apricots as indicated above.
2. Remove the seeds from the cardamom pods and pound to a powder.
3. Chop up the onion and garlic and sweat down in a little oil. Add the lentils, apricots and cooking liquid. Simmer for 40 minutes. Halfway through cooking, add the crushed cardamom seeds.
4. Remove from the heat for a few minutes before stirring in some yoghurt. Blend in the food processor. Add more seasoning and yoghurt if necessary. This soup can be served hot or chilled.

Gazpacho

Every region of Spain has variations of this cold summer soup, but the ingredients below are fairly standard. This Miriam Polunin recipe has the interesting addition of toasted hazelnuts. The advantages of this soup are that it is very low in fat and salt, and no heat-labile nutrients are lost in the cooking process. However scrupulous care must be taken, firstly in cleaning the vegetables and finally in chilling the soup, so that the possibility of bacterial contamination is minimised.

Ingredients   **5 portions**

400 gm tomatoes   1 clove of garlic
½ litre tomato juice (salt- and   25 ml tarragon vinegar
sugar-free)   1 tablespoon of fresh herbs such as
½ cucumber   parsley, chervil or tarragon
200 gm red peppers   10 gm hazelnuts
100 gm onion

Nutritional analysis per portion

Energy: 51 KCals
Fibre: 3 g
Fat: 1 g

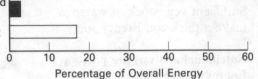

Method

1. Reserve a little of each vegetable for garnish and cut into the desired shape or dice.
2. Skin and de-seed the tomatoes, and de-seed the peppers. Roughly chop all the vegetables, and liquidise with half the tomato juice for 2–3 minutes. Gradually add the rest of the juice and the vinegar.
3. Refrigerate and serve with a garnish of fresh herbs, vegetables and toasted hazelnuts.

Jerusalem Artichoke Soup

Jerusalem artichokes have enjoyed something of a renaissance in recent years, being appreciated for their distinctive nutty flavour. The fact that there is no need to peel them means that minimal nutrient loss is incurred during preparation.

Ingredients   **4 portions**

750 gm Jerusalem artichokes   300 ml water or vegetable stock
100 gm onion   seasoning
15 gm polyunsaturated margarine   50 gm Greek yoghurt
700 ml skimmed milk   4 slices wholemeal bread

Nutritional analysis per portion
Energy: 222 KCals
Fibre: 3 g
Fat: 5.5 g

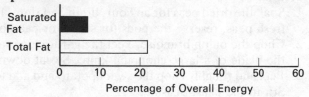

Method
1. Scrub the artichokes under running water.
2. Cut up the onion brunoise and sweat down in the margarine. Roughly chop the artichokes and add to the onion, along with the cooking liquid. Simmer for 30 minutes.
3. Remove from the heat for a few minutes, stir in the yoghurt and liquidise. Reheat and serve with toasted wholemeal croutons.

Pea and Yam Soup

Sweet potatoes are part of the yam family which were known to the Incas of Peru long before the Spanish arrived in the sixteenth century. They used to freeze the potatoes in the snow of the Andes, then allow them to thaw and squeeze out the juice. So it becomes apparent that not only are potatoes an ancient staple food, but that the 'modern' technique of preservation by freeze-drying has its origins way back in history.

Ingredients   **5 portions**
225 gm split green peas (or a pro-   2 leaves of mint
portion of fresh peas)   vegetable or hock stock
300 gm sweet potato   150 ml dry white wine
2 cloves of garlic   20 ml sunflower oil
150 gm onion

Nutritional analysis per portion
Energy: 249 KCals
Fibre: 9 g
Fat: 5 g

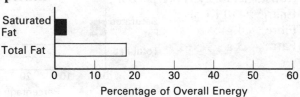

Method
1. Soak the dried peas for an hour, drain and rinse. If using a proportion of fresh peas, reserve the pods for stock, or pea pod soup.
2. Chop the onion brunoise. Peel the garlic cloves and roughly crush with the blade of a large chopping knife. Sweat down in the oil.
3. Peel and roughly chop the sweet potato and add to the onion and garlic. Stir in the peas. Season.
4. Pour over the wine and enough stock to cover the ingredients; this is intended to be quite a thick soup. Stock from hock bones will provide extra flavour, but be careful to skim off the surface fat. Drop in the mint leaves and bring the soup to a simmer. Cook for 40 minutes, under cover.
5. Remove the garlic and mint leaves. Liquidise and serve.

Watercress Soup

Watercress is so packed with vitamins and minerals that it is worth finding better ways of using it than the normal limp old garnish at the side of the plate. The lime, sorrel and watercress provide a fresh, sharp taste; the idea of adding lime juice derives from a Raymond Blanc recipe. Blanc epitomises so much that is good in modern cuisine – lightness, imagination and a striving for perfection. If you find you have a little money to spend, treat yourself to his book or, better still, a meal at 'Le Manoir aux Quatr' Saisons' in Oxfordshire.

Ingredients   **4 portions**
1 litre vegetable stock   300 gm watercress
100 gm onion   100 gm low-fat yoghurt
250 gm potato   10 ml olive oil
juice of 1 lime

Nutritional analysis per portion
Energy: 110 KCals
Fibre: 4 g
Fat: 3 g

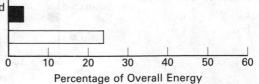

Method
1. Make a vegetable stock, if possible using some fresh chives and sorrel leaves.
2. De-stalk the watercress, wash and drain.
3. Slice the onion brunoise, peel and cube the potatoes. Sweat down in a little olive oil. When softened add the stock. Meanwhile, roughly chop the watercress and add it when the soup begins to boil. Simmer for no more than 10 minutes.
4. Stir in the lime juice and yoghurt off the heat. Liquidise thoroughly. Adjust for seasoning and gently bring back to the heat for service.

Note: Consume within 24 hours as the brilliant green colour fades rapidly.

Fish Broth

The relatively cold waters of Northern Europe may not provide the essential ingredients for classical dishes such as 'bouillabaisse' and 'bourride', but this should in no way prevent the making of a perfectly good fish soup. This recipe uses bream, for its distinctive flavour, but monkfish, cod, sole or halibut would do equally well. The red pepper provides a plentiful amount of vitamin C, as well as contributing towards the auburn hue of the finished dish.

Ingredients   **4 portions**

750 gm bream   *For the stock*
200 gm red peppers $1\frac{1}{2}$ litres water
100 gm onion   fish bones of the bream
2 cloves of garlic   juice of $\frac{1}{2}$ lemon
1 litre fish stock   150 gm onion
50 ml cognac   10 ml olive oil
bouquet garni (of orange zest,   peppercorns, bayleaf
fresh tarragon and 2 cloves)
20 ml olive oil
half a wholemeal baguette

Nutritional analysis per portion

Energy: 291 KCals
Fibre: 4 g
Fat: 8.5 g

	0	10	20	30	40	50	60
Saturated Fat	■						
Total Fat							

Percentage of Overall Energy

Method
1. Fillet the fish and make a stock with the ingredients outlined above. Skim thoroughly, and finally strain the stock.
2. Finely chop the onion, garlic and red pepper and sweat down in the oil. Add the cognac and cook fiercely for one minute to drive off most of the alcohol. Add the stock and bouquet garni and simmer for 15 minutes.
3. Add the sliced fish and cook for a further 15 minutes.
4. Liquidise and serve with slices of wholemeal baguette.

Coriander Soup

The name 'coriander' derives from the Greek, koris, a bug, there supposedly being a similarity between the smell of its green leaves and that of bed bugs! Not a very auspicious beginning, but perhaps in this instance the 'wisdom' of ancient Greece should be discounted, as both the aroma and flavour of coriander are most pleasant. Fortunately, supplies of the fresh herb are now widely available in the United Kingdom.

Ingredients   **5 portions**
400 gm onions   large bunch of fresh coriander
2 cloves of garlic   seasoning
350 gm potatoes   15 ml olive oil
$1\frac{1}{4}$ litres fresh vegetable stock

Nutritional analysis per portion
Energy: 117 KCals
Fibre: 3 g
Fat: 3.3 g

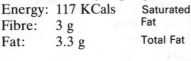

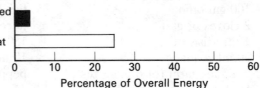

Percentage of Overall Energy

Method
1. Peel the onions and garlic and cut brunoise. Peel and roughly chop the potatoes; if using new potatoes they only need a good scrub rather than peeling.
2. Sweat down the vegetables in a little oil. Add the vegetable stock, bring to the boil and allow to simmer gently for 30 minutes.

3. Remove the stalks from the coriander and roughly chop the leaves. Add to the soup, covered and off the heat to allow the flavour to infuse. After 5 minutes, pass through the food processor. Serve with a sprig of fresh coriander leaves.

Vegetarian Dishes

For many years nutritional policy centred upon ensuring an adequate intake of protein in order to prevent certain 'deficiency diseases'. Meat, as a prime source of protein, was therefore considered an essential part of a balanced diet, and avoidance of meat was popularly associated with rather weakly creatures who must somehow have been lacking in red blood cells.

Today it is acknowledged that a selection of grains, vegetables and pulses provide vegetarians with quite sufficient protein, both in terms of quantity and quality. Furthermore such foodstuffs enjoy a healthy profile, being naturally rich in fibre and relatively low in fat.

Just as the nutritional perception of healthy food has changed, so has its culinary standing. It is no longer synonymous with tasteless stodge, but now encompasses light, succulent dishes and imaginative combinations of fruit and vegetables, colour and texture. A wealth of vegetarian cookery books are now available, some of which deserve special mention. Rose Elliot's books (Fontana), perhaps more than any others, have helped popularise and transform the image of vegetarian cooking. Colin Spencer (Thorsons) caters for both the vegetarian and the less committed 'demi-veg', that growing sector of the population which consumes a predominantly non-meat diet. Additionally, he is always quick to highlight practices which threaten the wholesomeness of the food supply. Madhur Jaffrey's *Eastern Vegetarian Cooking* (Cape) has its roots in the earliest vegetarian societies, and Time–Life's *Fresh ways with vegetables* provides an enticing selection of creative recipes.

The cyclical nature of vegetable and fruit crops allies vegetarianism with an important trend in modern cuisine – that of utilising the best of seasonal produce. Such an approach brings much more diversity, anticipation and enthusiasm to a kitchen, as is described here by Anton Mosimann:

> It is a great joy for our professional people, including myself, to create new dishes all the time. To get excited when you use good produce which maybe you haven't seen before, or which you know is coming into season next month; and you can't wait to get it and feel it again and

84

touch it, and then do something with it. I think that is very important (interview with the author at the Dorchester, October 1985).

A few of the recipes in this book, such as the 'Sweet and savoury vegetable ramekins', are specifically designed for Vegans. Many more can be simply adapted by replacing dairy products with soya ones, such as tofu, miso and soya milk. Unfortunately, many soya products are rather unappetising but, thankfully, new brands such as Tivall have been launched, which achieve a better taste without recourse to artificial preservatives or additives.

Couscous with Apricot Sauce

Couscous is a type of semolina, popular in North Africa and France. The cooking utensil – a couscoussier – is hard to come by in this country, but you can easily construct your own makeshift steamer with a sieve inside a covered pan of water.

In Morocco, couscous is often made with raisins, the steam rendering them plump and juicy. The taste can be improved by adding fresh herbs to the water, or mixing them with the grain itself. Really there is a limitless number of ways to impart extra flavour – mix in fruit, nuts, peas, peppercorns, mushrooms . . .

Ingredients   **4 portions**
500 gm couscous   50 gm raisins
100 ml vegetable stock   fresh parsley
250 gm dried apricots   fresh marjoram
$\frac{1}{2}$ lemon

Nutritional analysis per portion
Energy: 427 KCals
Fibre: 17 g
Fat: 1.3 g

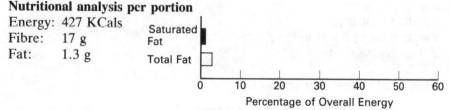

Method
1. Chop the apricots, barely cover with water, and soak for half an hour. Place them in a pan with the water they have soaked in. Season. Add a little vegetable stock and the juice of half a lemon. Simmer gently until softened. Finally blend in the food processor.
2. Meanwhile, mix the couscous, raisins and herbs, and place in the steamer. Sprinkle with water so that the couscous swells up slightly, and steam for 30 minutes. Sprinkle with a little more water, fluff up with a fork and continue steaming for a further half an hour.

3. Serve the couscous with the sauce and sprinkle generously with chopped parsley.

Carrot Gateau with Asparagus Sauce

This 'minceur' recipe uses very simple ingredients that are enhanced by the delicate flavours of gruyère and chervil. Carrots are famous for their vitamin A in the form of carotene but also offer useful amounts of B vitamins and vitamin E. Mushrooms contain virtually no fat and only 13 kilocalories per 100 gms. They provide some protein and iron, and more riboflavin and nicotinic acid than most other vegetables. Some knowledge of the countryside would allow us to benefit from the extensive range of wild mushrooms that grow in Britain: they possess a flavour far superior to the normal shop-bought variety. Dried ceps, morels and chanterelles can be obtained at some delicatessens, but only at an exorbitant price.

Ingredients   **4 portions**

600 gm carrots   2–3 eggs (enough to bind the other
15 gm sunflower margarine   ingredients)
1 teaspoon of clear honey   25 gm gruyère
130 gm mushrooms   fresh chervil
1 shallot

Asparagus Sauce
300 gm of asparagus
a little seasoning and nutmeg
100 ml vegetable stock

Nutritional analysis per portion
Energy: 149 KCals
Fibre: 6 g
Fat: 8 g

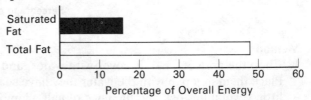

Method
1. Preheat the oven to 190°C, gas mark 5. Grease a small soufflé dish with a little margarine and line the base with greaseproof paper.

2. Scrub the carrots and slice into rings. Place in a small pan, barely half cover with water, and simmer with the honey, until virtually all the liquid has evaporated. Turn out into a bowl and, when cool, reserve the remaining cooking liquor and roughly chop the carrots.
3. Finely dice the mushrooms and shallot and sweat down briefly.
4. Beat the eggs with the grated gruyère, chopped chervil and a little seasoning. Mix all the ingredients together and fill the soufflé dish. Cook in a bain-marie, first covered with aluminium foil for 20 minutes, then uncovered until the mixture is almost firm. Leave to cool for 5 minutes, ease round with a knife, and turn out.
5. If using fresh asparagus, remove the woody stalks and tie the asparagus into a bunch. Stand the bottom half of the asparagus in water and poach for a few minutes until slightly softened. Remove the bundle and steam until tender. Liquidise, thinning if necessary with a little vegetable stock.
   If using the tinned product, simply drain and liquidise. Generally tinned asparagus comes in salted water, so be careful not to over-season.
6. Slice the gateau and serve with the asparagus sauce.

Blini with Red Pepper Topping

This recipe combines two diverse influences. The blini are pancakes of Russian origin, smaller and thicker than French crêpes. They are made from buckwheat flour, which is gluten-free, rather grey in colour and possessing a distinctive grainy texture. Traditionally in *haute cuisine*, blini are served with caviar, as they were in the award-winning film *Babette's Feast*. The red pepper mixture is derived from a Raymond Blanc recipe.

Ingredients   **4 portions**

Blini   *Red pepper topping*
120 gm buckwheat flour   60 gm onion
8 gm fresh yeast   100 gm tomatoes
1 egg   350 gm red peppers
150 ml skimmed milk   10 ml olive oil
75 ml water   50 ml white wine vinegar
1 teaspoon of honey   100 ml low-fat set yoghurt
                                         pinch of cayenne pepper

Nutritional analysis per portion
Energy: 193 KCals
Fibre: 4 g
Fat: 5.2 g

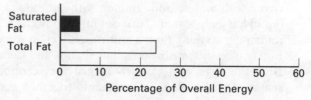

Percentage of Overall Energy

Method
Topping
1. Chop the onion brunoise, concasse the tomatoes and de-seed and dice the red peppers.
2. Sweat down the onion in a little olive oil, add the peppers, tomato, cayenne and seasoning, and cook out for five minutes at a brisk heat, stirring occasionally. Puree and return to the heat until most of the liquid has evaporated.
3. Reduce the wine vinegar by half and stir into the puree mixture. Allow to cool a little and fold in the yoghurt.

Blini
1. Whisk the honey with some of the warm water and stir in the yeast.
2. Combine the yeast mixture with the remaining water and the warmed milk. Gradually incorporate this with the egg yolk and flour until you have a fairly thick batter. Cover with a damp cloth and leave in a warm place for 45 minutes.
3. Fold in the stiff egg white. Place a tablespoonful of the batter in a warm crêpe pan and cook at a low heat for 4–5 minutes on each side, until lightly browned. Keep warm on a bain-marie.
4. To serve, smooth the red pepper topping onto the warm blini. Garnish with thin strips of blanched cucumber skin. This dish may be accompanied by the plum and raspberry vinegar sauce described on p. 90.

Pistou Ragout

This is a thicker version of the traditional Provençal dish 'Soupe au Pistou'. The essential ingredients of the pistou – olive, garlic and fresh basil – are central to cuisine in both Provence and Italy. The curative properties of garlic and basil have long been documented, but it is the protective effect of foods such as olive oil, containing predominantly monounsaturated fatty acids, that is now considerd responsible for the relatively low incidence of heart disease in Mediterranean countries.

Ingredients   **6 portions**

230 gm dried haricot beans   1 ½ litres vegetable stock
100 gm *each* of onion, carrot and   50 gm wholemeal spaghetti
potato   10 ml sunflower oil
200 gm courgettes   100 gm Edam cheese
250 gm tomatoes   1 wholemeal French stick (ba-
100 gm French beans   guette)

For the pistou
5 cloves of garlic
30 ml olive oil
1 bunch of fresh basil

Nutritional analysis per portion

Energy: 394 KCals
Fibre: 18 g
Fat: 12.8 g

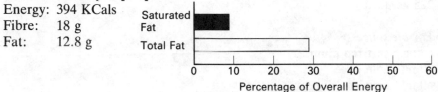

Method

1. Soak the haricot beans overnight. Cook in the vegetable stock, till tender, reserving the cooking liquor.
2. Dice the onion brunoise. Slice the courgettes. Scrub and roughly chop the potatoes and carrots. Top and tail the French beans and cut to 3 cm length. Skin and quarter the tomatoes.
3. Sweat down the onions, then gradually add the carrots, potatoes, French beans, courgettes, and lastly the tomatoes. Pour in the haricot beans, along with their cooking liquor. Simmer for 40 minutes. Towards the end of cooking add the spaghetti, broken up small.
4. To make the pistou, chop the garlic with a little salt and pound it, together with the basil. Add the olive oil and stir into the soup 5 minutes before serving.
5. Accompany with a sprinkling of grated cheese and toasted slices of wholemeal baguette.

Sweet and Savoury Vegetable Ramekins

This Vegan dish combines naturally sweet vegetables – carrot, parsnip and mangetout – with a tart plum sauce. It also makes use of two soya bean products, tofu and soy sauce. Most soy sauces contain a lot of additives, but at a slightly higher price you can buy brands, such as 'Kikkoman', which use no additives or sugar.

Ingredients   **6 portions**

500 gm spinach	1 bunch fresh coriander
150 gm mangetout	1 teaspoon clear honey
450 gm parsnip	30 ml soy sayce
450 gm carrot	20 ml olive oil
225 gm tofu	

For the sauce
400 gm tart red plums
40 ml apple juice
40 ml raspberry vinegar

Nutritional analysis per portion
Energy: 165 KCals
Fibre: 11 g
Fat: 5.3 g

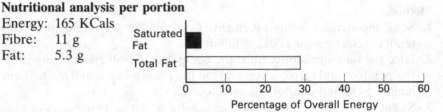

Method
1. Set the oven to 190°C, gas mark 5, and lightly brush six ramekin dishes with olive oil.
2. Pick the spinach and blanch for 30 seconds. Immerse in cold water and drain. Pull of the stringy bits of the mangetout and repeat the blanching operation.
3. Peel or scrub the carrots and parsnips and top and tail. Lightly brush a baking tray with oil and warm in the oven. Slice the parsnips lengthways, arrange on the baking tray, lightly baste and bake in the oven till lightly browned and tender.
4. Slice the carrots, chop the coriander and place in a saucepan. Merely half cover with water, add the honey and cook until almost all the liquid has evaporated.
5. Incorporate the soy sauce with the tofu and a little seasoning. Blend the carrots, remaining cooking liquor and one dessertspoonful of the tofu mixture in a food processor. Set aside. Now blend the roast parsnips and the remaining tofu.

6. Line the ramekins with spinach leaves, taking care to leave a good overlap. Spoon in a layer of the parsnip mixture and press down. Next arrange a layer of mangetout and finally the carrot mixture. Fold over the spinach leaves and cover each ramekin with aluminium foil. Bake in a bain-marie until set but still springy – approximately 25 minutes.
7. Meanwhile, de-stalk, wash and stone the plums, and gently simmer under cover, with the raspberry vinegar and apple juice, until the fruit has softened. Blend in the food processor with the cooking liquor.
8. To serve, warm the plum sauce and spoon onto white plates. Turn out the ramekins and decorate with tomato roses or julienne of red pepper.

Spinach and Pear Roulade

Roulades allow the chef to experiment with contrasting textures and flavours. In this dish the grainy texture of the pears contrast with the smooth spinach soufflé. An alternative piquant filling is suggested at the end, but really the choice of combinations is limitless.

Ingredients   **6 portions**
Roulade   *Filling*
1 kilo fresh spinach   750 gm ripe pears
4 egg yolks   30 ml cognac
7 egg whites   10 gm Flora margarine
nutmeg, seasoning   1 teaspoon of clear honey
15 ml sunflower oil

Nutritional analysis per portion
Energy: 139 KCals
Fibre: 2 g
Fat: 6.8 g

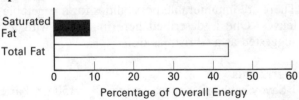

Method
1. Preheat the oven to 200°C, gas mark 6. Lightly oil a Swiss roll tin and line with a lightly-oiled sheet of greaseproof.
2. Pick and wash the spinach. Sweat down gently, merely using the water remaining on the spinach after washing. Cook out, under cover for a few minutes, stirring occassionally. When the spinach has softened and reduced in volume, turn out into a colander and, once cool, squeeze out the excess liquid.

3. Blend in a food processor with the egg yolks and seasoning.
4. Whisk the egg whites till stiff and fold a quarter of the whites into the spinach mixture. Combine this with the remaining whites, taking care not to lose aeration through being heavy-handed. (For tips on whisking egg whites, see p. 121.) Pour into the lined Swiss roll tin. Bake in the oven till set but springy – approximately 10 minutes.
5. Allow to rest for a few minutes and turn out onto a fresh sheet of greaseproof. Carefully peel off the original greaseproof, replace with a fresh sheet and roll up the roulade as you would a Swiss roll. Allow to cool.
6. Peel, quarter and core the pears. Finely dice and sweat down in the margarine and honey. Add the cognac and cook out gently under cover. When the pear is softened, pass or blend the mixture to a puree. Allow to cool.
7. Unravel the roulade, remove the greaseproof and spread with the pear mixture. Roll up again, removing the final sheet of greaseproof, and allow to 'set' for a few minutes. Serve in slices, either hot or cold.

Alternative fromage blanc filling
A simple but piquant filling can be made by finely dicing a few shallots, sweating down gently and combining with fromage blanc. To make your own fromage blanc, beat together equal quantities of cottage cheese and yoghurt with a little lemon juice. This roulade goes well with a tomato coulis.

Green Terrine

There are innumerable possibilities for a vegetable terrine bound in green leaves. One is described here in detail, with a further variation being suggested as a Christmas dish.

Ingredients   **6 portions**

1 Savoy cabbage, approximately   150 gm barley
750 gm   50 ml wine vinegar
1 clove of garlic   350 gm leeks
1 bunch of parsley   60 ml low-fat plain yoghurt
2 bunches of watercress (200 gm)   nutmeg, seasoning
200 gm potatoes   15 ml sunflower oil
4 egg yolks

For sauce
150 gm Greek yoghurt
1 bunch fresh coriander

Nutritional analysis per portion

Energy: 283 KCals
Fibre: 10 g
Fat: 9.6 g

Saturated Fat

Total Fat

| 0 | 10 | 20 | 30 | 40 | 50 | 60 |

Percentage of Overall Energy

Method

1. Set the oven to 180°C, gas mark 4.
2. Remove the stalks from the watercress and pick the parsley. Halve the cabbage and remove the hard central core. Peel or scrub the potatoes and cut into cubes.
3. Crush the garlic clove gently with the blade of a large knife, and remove the peel. Chop the leeks and sweat down with the garlic in a little oil. Set aside.
4. Poach the barley till tender, and mix in a bowl with the vinegar. Poach the potatoes for about 3 minutes. Drain and set aside.
5. Separate the large cabbage leaves and remove any thick stalks. Blanch these leaves in boiling water until supple – approximately 30 seconds. Drain, refresh in cold water and drain again. Leave to dry on a tea towel.
6. Shred the remaining cabbage, and either stir–fry along with the parsley and watercress, or blanch these ingredients briefly in very hot water. If blanching, strain and squeeze out the excess liquid.
7. Lightly oil a terrine or savarin mould and line with the large cabbage leaves. Leave a good overlap for folding over the filling.
8. Mix together all the vegetables and blend in the food processor for 60 seconds. Scrape down. Add the eggs, yoghurt and seasoning, and blend again until just short of a puree. Scrape out into a bowl, and stir in the barley.
9. Spoon this mixture into the mould and fold the overlapping green leaves on top. Cover with foil and bake in a moderate oven.
10. Chop the coriander and mix with the Greek yoghurt. When the terrine is set but still springy, turn out, slice and serve with a spoonful of coriander sauce.

Chestnut and Brussel Timbale with Carrot Sauce

A similar dish can be prepared for Christmas, using the seasonal ingredients of chestnuts and brussel sprouts. Chestnuts contain less calories than other nuts and are quite high in vitamins E and B$_6$. The sprouts should be poached till *al dente*, and the chestnuts roasted, peeled and roughly chopped. The sprouts, yoghurt and egg yolks are then blended in the food processor and mixed with the chopped chestnuts. This mixture is spooned into little moulds, which have been lined with blanched cabbage leaves. The moulds are then wrapped in foil and baked in a bain-marie. These little timbales go well with a pureed sauce of shallots, carrot and thyme.

Leek and Yoghurt Tartlets

This is simply an adaptation of the Provincial French dish 'Flamiche au poireau', substituting low-fat yoghurt for cream and using brown flour for the pastry. Food manufacturers are strenuously aiming to produce lower-fat margarines, and Proctor and Gamble have in fact developed a non-calorific fat substitute called 'Olestra'. It is a sucrose polyester which cannot be broken down by the digestive enzymes, and hence provides no calories. In the near future, then, it may well be possible to devise low-fat dishes using shortcrust pastry.

We are generally recommended to use just the white of leek, but most of the vitamin C lies within the green leaves, so try and use that part of the green which is not too rubbery. Jane Grigson sings the praises of this humble vegetable: 'The leek, once a poor joke against the Welsh, is now eaten in the highest gastronomic circles. And about time too, since its fine onion delicacy is underemployed in British cooking' ('A bulb for all seasons', *Observer magazine*, 11 Jan. 1987, p. 38).

Ingredients   **6 portions**
Pastry   *Filling*
250 gm wholemeal flour   1 kilo leek
120 gm polyunsaturated margarine   80 gm low-fat yoghurt
a little water   60 gm Greek yoghurt
                                     nutmeg, seasoning
                                     15 ml sunflower oil

Nutritional analysis per portion

Energy: 368 KCals
Fibre: 9 g
Fat: 20.6 g

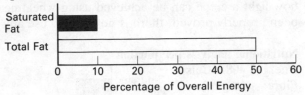

Saturated Fat
Total Fat

Percentage of Overall Energy

Method
1. Set the oven to 190°C, gas mark 5. To make the pastry, sift the flour and return the bran to the bowl. Rub the margarine and flour between your fingertips until well combined, and add a little cold water: just enough to be able to knead the ingredients into a ball. Wrap in clingfilm and rest in the fridge for 40 minutes.
2. Lightly oil six tartlet dishes (9 cm or 3½″ in diameter). Roll out the pastry and line the dishes. Prick the bases with a fork, rest for a further 30 minutes in the fridge, and bake blind for approximately 15 minutes.
3. Slice, wash and drain the leeks. Sweat down in a little oil till soft, and stir in the nutmeg and seasoning. Finally, fold in the yoghurt, fill the tartlets and serve warm.

Pancake Gateau

This is a many-tiered pancake dish: several layers of pancake with alternate fillings of lentil, tomato and spinach, finally topped with a cheese sauce and cooked till brown in the oven.

Lentils, like all members of the pulse family, are extremely rich in fibre and the B vitamins, especially nicotenic and panthonenic acids. They also provide good amounts of vitamins A, C and E. Spinach contains the same range of vitamins, as well as calcium and assorted minerals. Its iron – the source of Popeye's strength – cannot easily be absorbed by the body, but combining with a little lemon juice offers the best chance of doing so.

The béchamel for the cheese sauce is made from sunflower oil, wheatmeal flour and skimmed milk. Edam and fresh Parmesan are used, the former for its relatively low fat content, the latter for its incomparable flavour.

Wheatmeal pancakes
The secret is to have a hot crêpe pan. The batter should be swilled round the pan to a wafer-thin consistency, returned to a high heat, tossed over and finished. For immediate use the pancakes could be kept warm on a bain-marie; otherwise, once cooked, they lend themselves perfectly to

chilling or freezing, for consumption at a later date. You may be surprised how light a crêpe can be achieved using wheatmeal flour. If the pan has been properly proved, there is no need to use any oil at all.

Nutritional analysis per portion
Energy: 408 KCals
Fibre: 10 g
Fat: 14.4 g

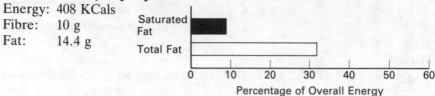

Percentage of Overall Energy

Batter (10–12 crêpes)
120 gm wheatmeal flour
1 large egg
300 ml skimmed milk

Method
Sift the flour and return the bran to the bowl. Beat in the egg and gradually incorporate the milk until a smooth batter is obtained. Leave in the fridge for an hour before using.

Lentil filling
250 gm green lentils
150 gm medium onions
1 clove of garlic

$\frac{1}{4}$ teaspoon Marmite
10 ml sunflower oil

Method
Soak the lentils for an hour, drain and rinse. Place in a saucepan, cover with cold water and cook until tender, stirring the Marmite into the cooking liquor. Chop the onions and garlic brunoise. Sweat down in the oil, stir in the lentils and, if necessary, add a little of the lentil cooking liquor. Cook out gently, under cover, for 10 minutes.

Tomato filling
1 bunch fresh basil
1 kilo tomatoes
180 gm medium onions

2 cloves of garlic
10 ml sunflower oil

Method
Prepare a cooked tomato concasse, sweating down the onions and garlic, and adding the quartered, skinned tomatoes and perhaps a little water. Add the roughly chopped basil shortly before the end of cooking.

Spinach filling

1.3 kilos spinach
nutmeg

120 gm low-fat yoghurt
1 lemon

Method

Pick the spinach, wash and drain. Sweat down gently in a covered pan, using only the liquid retained from the washing procedure. Stir occasionally, adding season and nutmeg. When cooked, leave to drain and squeeze out the excess liquid. Roughly chop and combine with the yoghurt and lemon juice

Cheese Sauce

40 ml sunflower oil
40 gm wheatmeal flour
600 ml skimmed milk

60 gm Edam
60 gm *fresh* Parmesan

Method

Gently heat the oil and add enough flour to make a roux consistency. Cook out for a couple of minutes. Gradually stir in the milk and simmer for 15 minutes. Stir in the grated cheese, off the heat.

Completion

Build up layers of pancake, spread alternatively with the three different fillings. Pour over the cheese sauce and bake in a moderate oven until nicely gratinated. Slice and serve.

Fish and Lean Meats

Fish have been described as the 'original convenience health food', as they are so nutritious and simple to cook. White fish are extremely low in fat, and most oily fish, such as sardines, herring and mackerel, are especially rich in the essential fatty acids, Omega-3 and Omega-6, which help protect the circulatory system.

Following the 1960s and the growth of supermarkets and convenience foods, a whole generation of people seemed virtually to miss out on the enjoyment of fresh fish, their experience confined almost entirely to rather anaemic slabs of packaged, frozen produce. In recent years, however, fresh fish sales have increased and many large retail chains are opening up their own wet fish counters. The variety of fish now on offer is much more enterprising, with fish farming making trout and salmon readily available, and air freight winging in the ingredients for a bowl of bouillabaisse or a marinade of sashimi. Wherever possible, though, the fresher and more immediate the catch, the better.

Whilst the NACNE Report recommended a shift in sources of protein from meat to plant produce, there is no requirement to abstain altogether from meat when following a healthy diet. Chapter 2 outlines the leaner varieties that can be selected, most of which are becoming increasingly popular (pp. 15–16). Consumption of chicken has increased steadily in recent years, and demand for venison looks set to rise dramatically during the 1990s. As game becomes more popular, it is important that the Meat Inspection Regulations should be extended to encompass these hitherto 'rare' meats; otherwise their hygienic quality cannot be guaranteed. Also it is to be hoped that the temptation to 'intensify' deer farming – with compound protein feeds, confinement and herding to market – will be resisted.

Recent research has shown organically reared cattle to have a healthier fat profile than their intensively reared counterparts. Just as important, perhaps, is the commonly held judgement that organic meat *tastes* much better. Animals at the Youngs' organic farm in Worcestershire are allowed to graze in family groupings, and when finally taken to slaughter are escorted calmly and individually, so that they do not produce the adrenalin which darkens and spoils the flesh. 'The result is beef the best this land can produce, both luscious and yielding plenty of juice, and with the kind of rich, pure, beef flavour which once made England's national dish the envy of the world.' (Lynda Brown 'Ahead of the herd' *A La Carte*, April 1988, p. 27)

Strudel Parcels of Salmon and Lime

Recently, questions have been raised concerning the wholesomeness of farmed salmon. The doubts relate to certain components of the fish feed, especially those colourings used to ensure that the flesh develops the desired pink hue. Wild salmon, although more expensive, are obviously exempt from such concern. Salmon, like all 'oily fish' – trout, herring, mackerel, etc. – inevitably contain a considerable amount of fat, but that fat is rich in the essential polyunsaturated fatty acids which help protect against heart disease.

Ingredients   **5 portions**

Strudel paste   *Filling and stock*
130 gm strong white flour   450 gm fresh salmon
1 egg   2 limes
30 ml skimmed milk   bunch of fresh lemon balm
10 ml olive oil   bayleaf, peppercorns, 50 gm onion
$\frac{1}{2}$ an egg (for egg wash)
Sauce
Either 300 gm rhubarb *or* 30 ml gazpacho

Nutritional analysis per portion
Energy: 277 KCals
Fibre: 4 g
Fat: 13.2 g

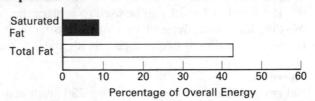

Method
1. Set the oven to 190°C, gas mark 5.
2. Fillet the salmon, cutting the flesh into five equal-sized portions. Set aside in the fridge.
3. Make a small amount of stock with the fish bones, roughly chopped lemon balm, peppercorns, bayleaf, brunoise of onion and enough water

to barely cover the ingredients. Bring to a simmer and cook gently for 20–30 minutes. Dégraissez.

4. Strain the stock, and reduce almost to a glaze. You only require enough liquid to moisten the salmon. When cool, add the juice of one lime, pour over the fish and leave in the fridge to marinate for an hour.

5. Wholemeal flour may be used for the strudel, but it will not produce a transparently thin pastry. Incorporate the egg into the flour and gradually beat in the milk and oil. Knead for several minutes, adding a little more flour if necessary, until you have a smooth dough. Leave to rest, covered on a floured surface, for 30–40 minutes.

6. Rolling the pastry requires a little patience at first, as the high gluten content of the flour makes for a very elastic dough. Roll the pastry out as thinly as possible into a rectangle.

7. Pick up the pastry and, with your fingertips or knuckles – whichever comes easier – carefully pull the strudel out from the middle to the edges, until you can see your hands through the pastry.

8. Trim off any uneven edges with a knife and cut the pastry into five equal pieces. Place a portion of salmon in the middle of each strip and fold into a parcel, using only enough pastry to enclose the fish; any excess should be cut away. Place on a lightly oiled baking tray, brush with egg wash, and bake in the oven for about 12 minutes. You want a nicely browned product, but if kept too long in the oven the fish will dry out. Garnish with twists of lime.

9. Serve with the stewed rhubarb, or simply the juice of the cooked rhubarb or, alternatively, with a coulis of gazpacho (p. 77).

Caribbean Cod

This recipe includes coconut products which are rather high in saturated fat. If desired, fish stock can be used to replace the coconut milk, but then the dish loses something of its authentic origins. Interestingly, the West Indian combiation of rice and peas is identical to the Italian 'risi e bisi'.

Ingredients   **4 portions**

500 gm cod fillets   230 gm tomatoes
4 king prawns   30 gm cashew nuts
200 ml fish stock   30 gm flaked almonds
100 ml coconut milk (either fresh   bunch of fresh coriander
or from a block of creamed coco-   15 gm desiccated coconut
nut)   3 cloves of garlic
125 gm onion   10 ml olive oil
1 tablespoon of chopped ginger

Nutritional analysis per portion

Energy: 396 KCals

Fibre: 9 g

Fat: 14.4 g

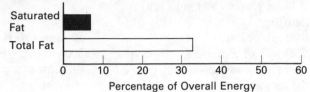

Method

1. Set the oven to 180°C, gas mark 4.
2. Shell the king prawns.
3. Chop the onion, garlic and ginger brunoise and sweat down in the oil. Skin and roughly chop the tomatoes and add to the onion mixture. Simmer with the coconut milk, fish stock and desiccated coconut for 20 minutes. Season.
4. Meanwhile, grill the nuts until they are lightly browned and roughly chop the coriander. Stir these into the vegetable mixture.
5. Cut the cod into portions and lay in a casserole dish or braising pan. Pour over the hot sauce and bake covered, in a moderate oven, for approximately 20 minutes. Add the king prawns shortly before completion, and serve one upon each dish.

For the rice accompaniment

120 gm brown rice

50 gm onion

60 gm peas

vegetable or fish stock (approximately twice the volume of rice)

40 gm dried kidney beans (optional)

If using the kidney beans, soak overnight, drain and rinse. Boil fiercely for 10 minutes, drain and rinse again. Cook in fresh water until tender. Simmer the rice gently in the stock, along with the brunoise of onion. Stir in the peas and kidney beans, and simmer gently until the liquid has been absorbed and the rice is tender. A little extra stock may be required.

Plaice Parcels

Any flat fish can be used for this recipe – lemon sole, dover sole, turbot – it all depends how much you are able to afford. The idea is to create a pocket inside the fish which you can fill with a flavoursome stuffing. You can experiment with different fish and various stuffings.

Ingredients　　　　　　　　　　　　　　　　　　　　　**4 portions**
2 large plaice (500 gm each)
Stuffing　　　　　　　　　　　　　　　　*Stock*
100 gm onion　　　　　　　　　　　　　500 gm fish bones
2 cloves of garlic　　　　　　　　　　　200 ml dry white wine
450 gm tomatoes　　　　　　　　　　　$\frac{1}{2}$ a lemon
10 ml sunflower oil　　　　　　　　　　bayleaf
80 gm fennel　　　　　　　　　　　　　peppercorns
　　　　　　　　　　　　　　　　　　　10 ml sunflower oil
　　　　　　　　　　　　　　　　　　　100 gm onion
　　　　　　　　　　　　　　　　　　　15 gm root ginger

Nutritional analysis per portion
Energy: 210 KCals
Fibre:　　3 g
Fat:　　　7.5 g

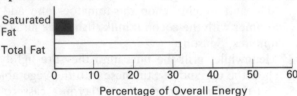

Method
1. Set the oven to 180°C, gas mark 4.
2. Prepare the stock. Sweat down the chopped onion and a teaspoon of chopped ginger in a little oil. Add the roughly scored fish bones and lemon juice, and sweat down gently for a few minutes under a cartouche. Add the bayleaf and peppercorns, and pour in the wine and enough water barely to cover the ingredients. Bring up to a gentle simmer and cook for 25 minutes. Dégraissez and strain.
3. To make the stuffing, finely chop the fennel, onion and garlic and sweat down in a minimum of oil. Add the skinned and roughly chopped tomatoes, and allow to cook out.
4. Cut off the heads of the fish. Using your fish filleting knife, carefully ease away the flesh from one side of the skeleton, taking care not to pierce the skin at the edge of the fillets. Having made a pouch, stuff the fish with the filling, lay in a sauteuse, and poach with the stock in the oven for approximately 12–15 minutes.
5. Fillet the fish and keep warm. Combine the cooking liquor and stuffing ingredients, and reduce to taste. Serve with the fish.

Monkfish and Almond Mousse

The British attitude towards monkfish has been transformed in recent years. Not so long ago, fishermen threw them back in the sea, as there was no market for them. Now their delicate flavour is highly rated and the price has gone up accordingly. They are a distinctly ugly fish paradoxically termed 'ange de mer' (angel of the sea) in France. Saffron is used in the rice accompaniment. It consists of the stigmas of the saffron crocus which have a unique flavour and strong yellow colour. In Greek mythology, the spice was accorded soporific properties; Venus used it to put her husband to sleep when she had a rendezvous to keep with Mars. Today it is extremely expensive because of the hard work involved in extracting the stigmas from the flowers. Powdered saffron is cheaper, but bears no resemblance to the genuine article.

Ingredients   6 portions

Mouse
1 kilo monkfish
150 ml dry white wine
200 gm onions
2 limes
½ teaspoon of chopped ginger
75 gm ground almonds
1 egg yolk
100 gm low-fat set yoghurt
25 gm flaked almonds
bayleaf, dill
10 ml olive oil

Sauce
600 gm tomatoes
200 gm onions
3 garlic cloves
fresh basil leaves
10 ml olive oil
Saffron rice
225 gm brown rice
100 gm onion
1 pack of *genuine* saffron
500 ml fish or vegetable stock

Nutritional analysis per portion
Energy: 430 KCals
Fibre: 7 g
Fat: 16.6 g

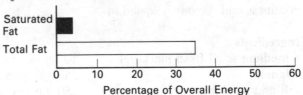

Method
1. Preheat the oven to 180°C, gas mark 4. Lightly oil a small terrine dish.
2. Remove the skin and stringy membrane from the monkfish tail and place, covered, in the oven, with the wine, diced onions and herbs. Cook until tender, approximately 20 minutes. Remove the bones and reserve the cooking liquor.
3. Blend the fish, ginger, egg yolk, juice of 1½ limes and ground almonds

in the food processor; fold in the yoghurt and cooking liquor. Taste and season accordingly.

4. Spoon into the terrine, cover with foil and return to the oven in a bain-marie. Cook until set but not dry. Turn out onto a platter and set aside.

5. For the saffron rice, dice the onion brunoise and poach in fish or vegetable stock along with the rice and saffron stamens. Approximately two and a half times the volume of the liquid is required to the amount of rice. When the rice is tender and has absorbed virtually all the stock, spoon into lightly oiled dariole moulds or little ramekins, and leave to set in the fridge.

6. Peel the garlic cloves and merely crush them roughly by leaning on them with the blade of a large chopping knife. During cooking, the garlic with render its flavour and can be discarded before liquidising the sauce. Sweat down the garlic and brunoise of onion. Add the concasse tomatoes and cook out gently for 15 minutes. Add the roughly chopped basil leaves and cook for a further ten minutes. Remove the garlic cloves and liquidise.

7. This dish can be served either hot or cold. Spoon a quantity of tomato sauce onto each plate, and upon it place a slice of the monkfish mousse. Turn out the rice moulds and locate judiciously on each plate. Decorate with toasted almonds and twists of lime.

Mackerel in Foil with Gooseberry Sauce

In this recipe, the tartness of the young gooseberries combines well with the mackerel. As with all methods of enclosed cookery, the food's natural goodness and flavour is sealed in.

Ingredients　　　　　　　　　　　　　　　　　　　　　**4 portions**

4 medium-sized fresh mackerel　　　10 ml olive oil
1 lemon　　　　　　　　　　　　　250 gm gooseberries
salt and black pepper　　　　　　　250 gm new potatoes
fresh tarragon and chervil　　　　　fresh chives

Nutritional analysis per portion
Energy: 417 KCals
Fibre:　5 g
Fat:　　27 g

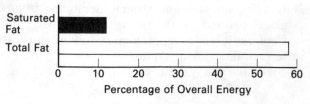

Method

1. Preheat the oven to 230°C, gas mark 8. Gut, wash and dry the mackerel and sprinkle the insides with lemon juice. Put a bunch of mixed herbs inside the cavity of each fish and brush the skin lightly with olive oil. Wrap each fish in foil and fold up tightly. Bake for 10 minutes.
2. To make the sauce, top and tail the gooseberries. Add a little water and simmer gently, under cover, until the fruit has softened. Blend in the food processor, season to taste, and serve with the fish.
3. For the accompanying potatoes, scrub under running water, poach or steam till tender, and serve sprinkled with chopped chives.

Deer Cutlets with Juniper Berries

Venison is a very lean meat and extremely economical to produce; ten beasts can be put to an acre of grass whereas beef cattle need an acre each. This adaptation of an Elizabeth David recipe uses roe deer, which is greatly valued for its wild flavour and tenderness.

Ingredients   **4 portions**

4 cutlets (180 gm each) from the   *Accompaniment*
best end of neck   500 gm sweet potato
half a lemon   15 gm polyunsaturated margarine
10 crushed juniper berries   50 ml skimmed milk
bunch of marjoram, seasoning
100 gm onion
100 gm carrot
100 ml dry white wine
100 ml game or chicken stock
15 ml sunflower oil
120 gm redcurrants
juice of $\frac{1}{2}$ a Seville orange

Nutritional analysis per portion

Energy: 453 KCals
Fibre: 7 g
Fat: 15 g

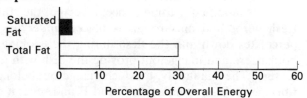

Method

1. Set the oven to 160°C, gas mark 3.
2. Rub the cutlets with the cut side of a lemon and squeeze on a little juice. Mix the juniper berries, chopped marjoram and seasoning, and rub this mixture into the cutlets. Leave for an hour in the fridge.
3. Sweat down the onion and carrot, remove from the sauteuse and set aside. Brown the cutlets and drain on kitchen paper. Arrange with the vegetables in a gratin dish. Deglaze the sauteuse with the wine and stock and pour over the cutlets. Cover with foil and bake in a low oven for 50 minutes or till tender.
4. Shortly before service, simmer the redcurrants in a little of the cooking liquor with a squeeze of orange juice. Set aside.
5. When cooked, remove the cutlets and strain and dégraisser the juices. This can either be served simply as a gravy, or pureed with the carrot and onion to make a vegetable sauce.
6. Accompany with the redcurrants and puree of sweet potato. Eliza Acton, the famous Victorian cook, recommended that sweet potatoes be cooked in their skins, so as to retain maximum flavour. After cooking and cooling a little, the skins can be removed and mashed with the margarine and milk.

Parslied Chicken

Parsley is a highly nutritious food, rich in iron, fibre and vitamin C. Purslane, a flat-leafed form of parsley, has quite remarkable qualities. A cookery book dating back to the time of Richard II claims that it 'doth extynct the ardour of lassyvyousness and mytygate great heat in all the inward parts of man'. Meanwhile, in Malawi, purslane has a name which means, 'buttocks of the wife of the chief'. More significantly, it is ranked as a superfood in combating heart disease. Purslane contains more Omega-3 fatty acids than any other vegetable yet analysed. Omega-3 fatty acids are believed to be important in preventing heart attacks, and in reinforcing the body's immunity to infection.

In this modified 'cuisine minceur' recipe, the stuffing of fromage blanc, fresh herbs and mushrooms is placed *under the skin*, and the flavour percolates down into the flesh during the cooking process. The pommes boulangère and mangetout provide the dish with a contrast of colour and texture. The pea family, to which mangetout belong, is well endowed with fibre, as well as vitamins A, C and E and several of the B complex.

Ingredients   **4 portions**
1 free-range chicken (1 kilo)   *Fromage blanc*
large bunch of fresh parsley   150 gm cottage cheese
fresh chives   150 gm low fat yoghurt
fresh marjoram   Juice of a lemon,
80 button mushrooms   Nutmeg. Seasoning
20 ml Arachide
Accompaniment
150 gm mangetout
350 gm potato
100 gm onion
2 cloves of garlic
150 ml chicken stock
150 ml skimmed milk

Nutritional analysis per portion
Energy: 361 KCals
Fibre: 8 g
Fat: 12.7 g

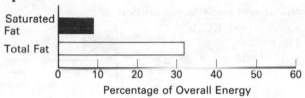

Method
1. Set the oven to 190°C, gas mark 5.
2. Beat together the ingredients for the fromage blanc. Work in the fine dice of mushrooms and the chopped herbs. Lift the skin away from the legs and breasts by carefully easing your index finger under the skin, and insert the stuffing. Reserve the remaining fromage blanc mixture for the sauce.
3. Season the inside of the bird, baste sparingly with hot arachide oil, cover with foil and roast in the oven.
4. For the accompanying vegetables, chop the onion and garlic to a fine brunoise. Peel the potatoes, or simply scrub under running water, and slice them thinly on a mandolin. Arrange layers of lightly seasoned potato in a small casserole dish, interspersed with the chopped onion and garlic. Warm the milk and stock and merely half cover the potatoes. Place in a moderate oven for 45 minutes or until golden brown. Briefly poach or steam the mangetout so that the crunchiness and colour is retained.
5. When cooked, remove the bird from the roasting pan, pour out the juice and skim off the fat. Return the dégraissé juices and the remaining fromage blanc mixture to the roasting pan. Bring to a simmer on top of the stove, stirring all the while, to incorporate the caramelised sediment at the bottom of the pan. This forms the basis for a tasty sauce.

6. Dissect the chicken into 4 portions, remove the skin and serve with the sauce and vegetables.

Rabbit in Plum Sauce

Ingredients   **4 portions**
1.2 kilos rabbit (jointed)   2 cloves of garlic
10 ml olive oil   fresh thyme and rosemary
500 gm purple plums   110 ml port
150 gm onion   1 clove

Nutritional analysis per portion
Energy: 341 KCals
Fibre: 4 g
Fat: 10 g

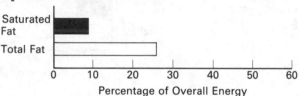

Percentage of Overall Energy

Method
1. 1. Preheat the oven to 160°C, gas mark 3.
2. Stone the plums. Slice the onions thinly and chop the garlic very fine.
3. Sauté the rabbit in olive oil. As soon as it is golden, drain on kitchen paper, to absorb the fat. Lay on the bottom of a casserole the onions and garlic, then the herbs and clove and finally the rabbit joints.
4. Deglaze the sauteuse pan with port and boil for 1 minute, stirring to take up the caramelized sediment stuck to the bottom of the pan. Pour the juices into the casserole, arrange the plums on top, cover and cook for 1 hour or until tender.
5. When cooked, remove the rabbit pieces and strain the remaining ingredients through a sieve for use as a sauce.

Pear and Calves' Liver Flower

Liver is rich in iron and zinc, as well as containing vitamin E and all the B vitamins. Calves' liver is very expensive but exquisitely tasty. Some healthfood customers, typically concerned for animal welfare, may baulk at the idea of eating calves' meat because of the notoriety surrounding their rearing conditions. However the Farm Animal Welfare Council recently scored a significant success when the farming ministry announced that it was going to ban the veal crate system, in which young calves are kept closely penned for several months.

This is a Jocelyn Dimbleby recipe. As well as providing an interesting contrast of flavour and texture, the visual presentation of this dish should be a picture:

a bed of spinach in the middle of the plate;
a fan of pear slices round the edge, interspersed with thin slices of liver;
finally topped with a flower of pear slices and a sprig of fresh mint.

Ingredients   4 portions

2 teaspoons ground coriander   650 gm fresh spinach
2 teaspoons paprika   nutmeg
2 pinches of cayenne   10 ml olive oil
300 gm calves' liver   juice of a lemon
400 gm ripe pears   fresh mint

Nutritional analysis per portion

Energy: 223 KCals
Fibre: 4 g
Fat: 10 g

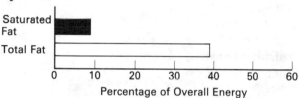

Method

1. Set the oven to 220°C, gas mark 7.
2. Pick and wash the spinach and cook in a covered pan, merely in the water the spinach retains after rinsing. Drain, cool and squeeze out the excess moisture. Roughly chop the spinach and combine with the nutmeg and juice of half a lemon.
3. Peel the pears and smear with lemon juice to stop discolouration.
4. Brush the liver with oil, sprinkle with peppers and spice, and wrap in foil. Place in a hot oven for 10 minutes, or until just pink inside.
5. Meanwhile, slice the pears thinly. Flatten the spinach into a circle in the middle of the plate.
6. Slice the calves' liver thinly. Then proceed to arrange the ingredients as outlined above.

Pheasant with Cider

This dish derives from Jane Grigson's account of 'Le Gros Souper' a traditional Provençal Christmas dinner. The birds should first have been hung for a week in a cool environment (4–7°C). During hanging microbes break down the tissue, tenderising the flesh and improving the flavour.

One writer in the *Guardian* Food and Drink page (11 Sept. 1987) described how he learnt to hang and prepare all forms of game over 50 years ago: 'The birds were hung to the customer's taste, then plucked, drawn and dressed. We used wooden skewers to set them up, breasts puffed out, wings set back like Guardsmen's shoulders. Cock pheasants tail feathers were left intact, and fanned, to be removed for cooking and replaced by the cook before going to the table.'

Ingredients   **4 portions**
a brace of pheasants   *Salad accompaniment*
15 ml olive oil   200 gm water cress
80 gm low-fat yoghurt   2 oranges
40 gm Greek yoghurt
800 gm Cox's orange pippins
100 ml cider
30 ml calvados

Nutritional analysis per portion
Energy: 503 KCals
Fibre: 6 g
Fat: 19 g

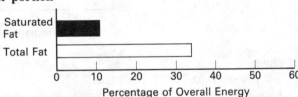

Percentage of Overall Energy

Method
1. Preheat the oven to 180°C, gas mark 4.
2. Heat the oil and brown the birds in a sauteuse. Remove the pheasants, season the insides and spoon in the yoghurt.
3. Peel, core and slice the apples and line the base of a casserole dish with half of them. Put the birds on top. Deglaze the sauteuse with the cider and calvados, scraping with a wooden spoon to incorporate any caramelized sediment, and pour over the birds. Cover with the remaining apples and cook, enclosed, in the oven for one hour.
4. Remove the birds and allow to rest before dissecting. Dégraissez the juices, and serve with the apples and a crisp watercress and orange salad.

Duckling with Honey and Lemon

Geese and ducks, although fatty beasts, are quite good sources of unsaturated fatty acids. Regular pricking of the skin during cooking will release a great deal of fat, and the skin can be removed prior to service. A new breed of duck, called Gressingham, is being reared in Cumbria. It is lower in fat, possesses the gamey flavour of the wild bird, and has a meat to bone ratio almost twice that of an Aylesbury duck.

Broccoli and carrots accompany this dish, not only to provide a pleasant contrast of colour, but also for their prime nutritional value. They are both excellent sources of vitamins A and C, and broccoli, like all leafy greens, is also rich in folic acid – a nutrient often lacking in the British diet, which is essential for avoiding anaemia.

This recipe comes from Leslie Forbes's outstanding book, *A Table in Provence* (Webb & Bower, 1987). It is full of enticing illustrations and anecdotes which capture the flavour and lifestyle of this region of France.

Ingredients   6 portions

2 young ducks with giblets
100 gm carrots
100 gm onions
thyme, bayleaf
300 ml dry white wine
100 ml wine vinegar
2 dessertspoons of clear honey
juice of 2 lemons

Vegetable accompaniment
400 gm carrots
400 gm broccoli

Nutritional analysis per portion

Energy: 352 KCals
Fibre: 5 g
Fat: 13.6 g

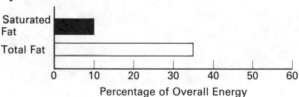

Method

1. Preheat the oven to 220°C, gas mark 7. Cut off the lower wings and place in a pan along with the giblets, vegetables and herbs. Pour in the wine and enough water to cover. Simmer for 45 minutes. The alcohol will be driven off when the sauce is reduced later. Dégraissez. Finally strain the stock.

2. Roast the duckling in the oven, allowing approximately 60 minutes, depending on the size of the birds. After 20 minutes' cooking, turn the heat down to 200°C, gas mark 6. Twice during cooking prick the skin all over to allow the fat to escape. Take care not to pierce the flesh.

3. Remove the birds and keep warm. Pour off the cooking liquor and allow to settle. Skim off the fat.
4. Cut the carrots into batons and the broccoli into florets, and poach or steam until *al dente*.
5. Deglaze the roasting tray with the wine vinegar and lemon juice. Add the honey, stock and skimmed roasting juices. Reduce until quite thick.
6. For service, remove the skin from the ducks. You should be able to get 3 portions from each bird: a half-fan of breast with each leg, plus a whole fan of breast. Serve upon the sauce, with the accompanying vegetables.

Salads

A telling indictment of English cookery is the acidulated fermenting salad of the eat-as-much-as-you-like bar. The shredded vegetation lives in a purgatory of vinegar, on a suspended sentence, until the next vanload arrives (Drew Smith, 'Renaissance of the salad', *Guardian*, p. 25, 15 Oct. 1988).

For too long, unappetising salads did little to enhance the image of healthy eating. A side plate of limp lettuce, bitter tomato and dry cucumber would probably be served totally unanointed, or accompanied by the standard little carton of processed 'salad cream'.

Thankfully recent years have seen the metamorphosis of salads into much more imaginative and flavoursome forms. This is a most welcome development, as there can be few more refreshing or nutritious components to a meal than a dish of fresh leaves, fruit and vegetables. Many catering establishments now guarantee the succulence of produce by nurturing their own little herb and salad patches, but even without this facility an extensive variety of fresh herbs and leaves is now readily available.

The hegemony of the iceberg lettuce has been broken. Today chefs can choose from a wide selection, such as oakleaf, frisée, lamb's lettuce, rocket, Lollo Rosso, Little Gem, Quatro Stagioni, escarole, batavia and radicchio. Likewise, the components of dressings are now more varied, with flavoursome oils such as peanut, olive and walnut, vinegars made from wines, cider and raspberries, and a range of different mustards.

The possible combinations of salads are almost infinite, so this chapter simply presents a collection of recipes based on particularly nutritious ingredients. Maximum nutrient retention will be achieved by using the freshest possible produce and keeping food preparation and cooking times down to a minimum. A further important factor determining the nutritional profile of a salad is the amount of dressing employed. Whilst the oils used in the two dressings below are both predominantly unsaturated, it can be seen that the mayonnaise in particular is extremely calorific: 360 ml

113

carries 2856 kilocalories and 313 gm of fat. Even the relatively 'low-fat' dressing, based principally on yoghurt and apple juice, contains 665 kilocalories and 61 gm of fat for every 340 ml. It becomes clear that, in healthy eating, dressings should be used in moderation.

Traditional Mayonnaise

Ingredients

300 ml sunflower oil   1 teaspoon of mustard
2 egg yolks   20 ml wine vinegar

Nutritional analysis
Energy: 2856 KCals
Fibre: 0 g
Fat: 313.3 g

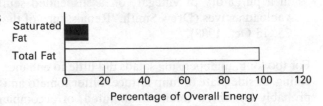

Method
1. Beat together the egg yolks, mustard and a little vinegar, and gradually whisk in the oil.
2. Season, taste and sharpen, if desired, with a little vinegar or lemon juice.

Yoghurt and Apple Juice Dressing

Mix all the following ingredients together:

60 ml olive oil   juice of 1 lemon
30 ml white wine vinegar $\frac{1}{2}$ teaspoon of French mustard
100 ml apple juice   125 ml low-fat yoghurt

Nutritional analysis
Energy: 665 KCals
Fibre: 0 g
Fat: 61.5 g

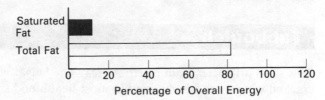

Sunshine Salad

This is an extremely simple, refreshing and nutritious dish to make. Carrots are rich in vitamin A and bananas are a good source of potassium. When concern is being expressed at the high salt content of many convenience products, it is especially important to eat foods rich in potassium in order to maintain the delicate equilibrium of sodium and potassium in the body.

The peanut is not in fact a nut at all but the seed of an annual legume. The peanut-bearing pods grow below the surface of the earth, hence the alternative name sometimes used: 'groundnuts'. Peanuts contain all 8 essential amino-acids, in addition to B vitamins, potassium, phosphorus, magnesium and calcium. They also provide a good deal of fibre; it is estimated that a generous peanut butter sandwich made with wholemeal bread supplies about half the recommended daily fibre intake. The fat profile is also favourable, with a 3 : 2 ratio of polyunsaturated to saturated fatty acids.

Ingredients   **5 portions**
500 gm carrots   50 gm peanuts
2 bananas   1 lemon
70 gm sultanas

Nutritional analysis per portion
Energy: 152 KCals
Fibre: 8 g
Fat: 5 g

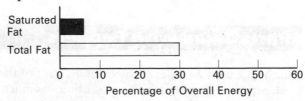

Method
1. Peel and grate the carrots.
2. Slice the bananas thinly and sprinkle with lemon juice.
3. Combine all the ingredients together.

Tabbouleh

This salad originates from North Africa. The bulgar wheat, also known as cracked wheat, can be obtained in most healthfood shops.

Ingredients   **5 portions**

125 gm bulgar wheat	40 ml lemon juice
1 bunch of parsley	400 gm tomatoes
1 bunch of *fresh* mint	50 gm spring onions
20 ml olive oil	30 gm radish

Nutritional analysis per portion

Energy: 142 KCals
Fibre: 2 g
Fat: 4.4 g

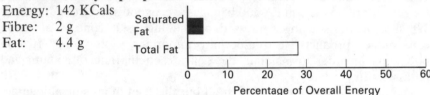

Method
1. Pour hot water over the bulgar wheat and leave to soak until the grains are tender – approximately 20 minutes. Drain, cool and squeeze out the excess water.
2. Chop the parsley finely.
3. Concassez the tomatoes and quarter.
4. Slice the radish and spring onions finely.
5. Whisk the oil and lemon with seasoning.
6. Combine all the ingredients. Snip in the mint with a pair of scissors. Chill and serve.

Pasta Salad with Peppers

Elizabeth Luard provides a colourful account of the nutritional virtues of fresh peppers. They contain 'up to six times as much vitamin C per drop of juice as lemons and oranges. They are also plentifully endowed with other good things including vitamin A, the source of carotene – which makes flamingo feathers pink, shrimps blush scarlet, gives the carrot its orange hue and enables good children who eat up their vegetables to see in the dark' (Elizabeth Luard, *European Peasant Cookery: the rich tradition'*, Bantam, 1986, p. 424).

Ingredients   **5 portions**
225 gm wholemeal pasta shells   250 gm tin of sweetcorn
80 gm green pepper   250 gm tomatoes
80 gm red pepper   fresh parsley

Nutritional analysis
Energy: 196 KCals
Fibre: 9 g
Fat: 1.5 g

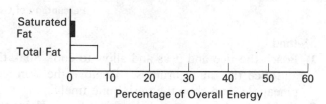

Percentage of Overall Energy

Method
1. Cook the pasta shells and refesh in cold water. Drain.
2. Dice the peppers finely and drain the sweetcorn. Remove the tomato
   skins and quarter. Combine all the ingredients together, sprinkle with
   chopped parsley, and serve with either a dressing or a tomato coulis.

Pawpaw in a Lime Juice Dressing

This recipe comes from Jean Conil's *Cuisine Végétarienne Française*
(Thorsons, 1985). It may come as a surprise to some people that a
vegetarian tradition actually exists in France! Too often there appears to be
an exasperating contrast between the rich quality and variety of vegetable
produce in French markets and the dominance of meat on restaurant
menus, with vegetables merely playing the supporting role of a garnish.

Walnut is the nut richest in linoleic acid, the essential polyunsaturate
that cannot be constructed in the body: 60% of oil in walnuts is linoleic and
11% the important linolenic. Walnuts also contain good amounts of fibre,
B vitamins and vitamin E.

Pawpaw, or papaya, is the source of the enzyme papain, which is used to
tenderise meat. Here we will be appreciating it for its smooth texture,
sweet flavour and delicate aroma.

Ingredients   **4 portions**
2 large pawpaws   60 gm chopped walnut
60 gm rice   50 gm raisins
60 gm peas   20 ml brandy
40 gm spring onion   2 limes (one for juice, one for
1 small pineapple   garnish)
60 ml low-fat yoghurt

Nutritional analysis per portion
Energy: 299 KCals
Fibre: 7 g
Fat: 8 g

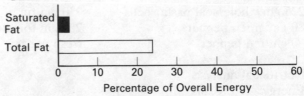

Method
1. Poach the rice and peas and allow to cool. Soak the raisins in brandy and dice the onion brunoise. Remove the skin and hard core of the pineapple, and chop the flesh quite finely.
2. Make sure the pawpaws are good and ripe. Halve them and remove the seeds. Combine all the ingredients in (1) with the yoghurt and chopped walnuts, and fill the pawpaws.
3. Pour over the lime juice and serve with twists of lime.

Beetroot, Celeriac and Beansprout Salad

Bean and seed sprouts are nutritionally valuable. They contain vitamin C and, once germination begins, develop several other vitamins, including B_{12}, which is often lacking in Vegan diets. The Arabs called alfalfa seeds the 'Father of all foods', attributing miraculous properties to them. Indeed they possess a higher protein content than beef or milk, and several of the obscure vitamins such as K and Y. Packs of mixed bean and seed sprouts are now available in many healthfood shops.

This salad provides a good contrast between the soft smooth texture of the beetroot and the crisp, crunchy celeriac and beansprouts.

Ingredients   **6 portions**
800 gm raw beetroot   250 gm celeriac
250 gm mixed bean and seed
sprouts

Nutritional analysis per portion
Energy: 57 KCals
Fibre: 5 g
Fat: 0.1 g

Method
1. Rinse the bean and seed sprouts in a colander.
2. Peel the celeriac and cut into batons. Michel Guérard refers to these as healthy 'chips'.
3. Clean the beetroot, remove the roots, but do not peel. Poach till tender – about 20–30 minutes.
4. Drain, cool and peel. Cut into slices or batons. Toss all the ingredients together, and combine with either a dressing or the vinaigrette used for the chicken liver salad (see below).

Salade Tiède de Foie de Volaille

The 'salade tiède' has its origins in the provincial heritage of Burgundy, Champagne and the Loire. A selection of fresh shoots or leaves would be gathered and served with a warm vinaigrette, and a meat item – such as bacon, goose or chicken livers – tossed on top. Today, warm salads are identified with 'nouvelle cuisine' because the variety of salad leaves now available enable the chef to create an interesting amalgam of colours, shapes and textures.

This recipe uses chicken livers, firstly for their flavour, and secondly because they offer terrific nutritional value. Liver is a lean source of meat, extremely rich in iron, and also containing generous amounts of zinc, vitamins A and E and several vitamins of the B complex including the important B_{12}.

Ingredients   **4 portions**

200 gm chicken livers   *Vinaigrette*
100 ml medium dry sherry   30 ml walnut oil
30 gm hazelnuts   20 ml raspberry vinegar
100 gm frisée lettuce $\frac{1}{2}$ teaspoon grainy mustard
100 gm lamb's lettuce   juice of $\frac{1}{2}$ lemon
100 gm oakleaf lettuce
100 gm radicchio
250 gm new potatoes

Nutritional analysis per portion
Energy: 257 KCals
Fibre: 3 g
Fat: 14 g

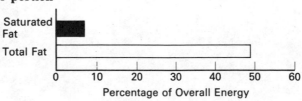

Method

1. Clean the chicken livers, removing any discoloured parts. Place in a bowl with the sherry, and leave to marinate in the fridge for a couple of hours.
2. Scrub the potatoes under the tap; poach until tender. Cool and slice into cubes.
3. Wash and drain the salad leaves, and arrange artistically around the 4 plates.
4. Grill or roast the hazelnuts until lightly brown and rub between your hands to remove most of the skin. Scatter among the leaves, along with the cubed potatoes.
5. Drain the chicken livers and sauté for 3–4 minutes in a non-stick pan. As they are cooking, whisk together the ingredients for the vinaigrette. When the livers are done, toss onto the salad plates, quickly swill the vinaigrette round the pan, sprinkle over the leaves and serve.

Healthy Desserts

Many people make a valiant effort to eat healthily when they go out for a meal, but succumb totally when it comes to the dessert course. All their good intentions fly out of the window as they guzzle down oodles of cream, lashings of syrup and thick coatings of chocolate. So the challenge exists to produce appetising and appealing recipes that are rich in fibre, and low in fat and added sugar.

All the sweetening in this book comes from fruit and honey. Although honey is not greatly different in nutritional content from refined sugar, it does have several advantages. First, it is approximately twice as sweet as sugar, thus requiring less lavish application; second, it contains trace amounts of fibre and minerals; and third, it now comes in varieties – such as lavender and acacia – which retain the delicate perfume of the flower nectar from which it derives. Honey is not easy to quantify precisely, and the amount suggested in each recipe may be modified according to the natural sweetness of the accompanying ingredients.

In the past, much of healthy cuisine was typified by rather heavy dishes. To avoid this, many of the recipes here use aerated egg whites to provide the desired lightness. There are several tips worth adopting when whisking egg whites:

1. Make sure that all equipment is scrupulously clean, dry and free from grease.
2. Begin whisking at a moderate speed, before increasing momentum.
3. Add a little salt or lemon juice during whisking. This helps to increase the stability of aerated egg whites during cooking.
4. Avoid whisking the whites too far, as a totally dry foam becomes very difficult to incorporate. Achieving soft peaks is generally quite sufficient.
5. When combining the stiff egg whites into the main ingredients of a recipe, merely cut them in with a large metal spoon. There is no need to continue this cutting motion until all the whites have been incorporated to an absolute smoothness; that way much of the aeration and

121

lightness is lost through overworking. At all costs, avoid stirring or beating the whites into the mixture.

6.   Incorporate a quarter of the whites into the main ingredients to start with. Then combine this mixture with the remaining three-quarters.

In the two recipes which require a setting agent, agar-agar can be used instead of gelatine. It is seaweed-based and therefore acceptable to vegetarians. For those Vegans who do not use honey, sweetening can be provided by using additional amounts of pureed dried fruit.

Exotic Fruit Terrine with Mango Coulis

Ingredients   **6 portions**
3 bananas   400 ml unsweetened orange juice
$\frac{1}{2}$ galia melon   2 mangos
3 kiwi fruit   2 passion fruit
2 oranges   6 leaves gelatine
1 pawpaw

Nutritional analysis per portion
Energy: 194 KCals
Fibre: 7 g
Fat: 0.5 g

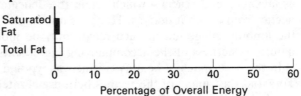

Method
1.   Soak the gelatine in a little water. Fill a small terrine with water and place in the fridge.
2.   Peel and slice the kiwi fruit. Slice the bananas thinly lengthways. Halve the melon and pawpaw, remove the seeds, cut away the peel and once again slice the fruit thinly lengthways. Remove the peel and pith from the oranges and cut into segments. Reserve the juice from the pulp.
3.   Pour out the water from the terrine and line the base with kiwi fruit. Cut the banana, melon and pawpaw slices into lengths that fit neatly inside the terrine. Arrange first the banana slices on top of the kiwi, then the melon, followed by the pawpaw. Lastly arrange the orange segments on top.
4.   Bring the orange juice to the boil. Drain the gelatine and whisk in. When tepid, pour over the fruit and chill to set.

5. Meanwhile, peel the mangos, remove the stones and liquidise the mango flesh. Scoop out the passion fruit and mix with the juice from the orange pulp. Pass all three ingredients firmly through a conical strainer. This is the coulis on which the slices of terrine will be served.
6. Before service, cut around the edges of the tin. Immerse the bottom briefly in hot water. Turn out. You should have a nice layered pattern of fruit. If the jelly is a little squishy, give a quick blast in the freezer before slicing.

Healthy Crumble

There are limitless combinations for the fruit fillings. In the autumn, freshly picked blackberries and apples produce a wonderful flavour. Here fresh pineapple is added to lightly stewed apples.

Ingredients   **5 portions**

Filling   *Topping*
1 kilo cooking apples   25 gm desiccated coconut
75 gm sultanas   50 gm sunflower seeds
1 tablespoon clear honey   50 gm sesame seeds
the flesh of half a large pineapple   50 gm wheatgerm
100 ml apple juice (unsweetened)   50 gm raisins
                                       100 ml apple juice

Nutritional analysis per portion
Energy: 379 KCals
Fibre: 10 g
Fat: 14.5 g

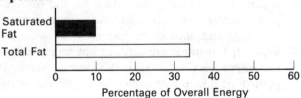

Method
1. Set the oven to 180°C, gas mark 4.
2. Peel, core and slice the apples. Place in a pan with the honey, sultanas and apple juice, and cook gently under cover. When the apple has softened, stir in chunks of pineapple. Line a pie dish with the fruit filling.
3. Combine all the topping ingredients together. Spread over the fruit. Bake until lightly brown.
4. This crumble goes well with the pineapple sorbet on p. 127.

Little Orange Custards

This simple recipe needs to be well chilled to produce a refreshing and delicate flavour. The orange is a good source of vitamin C, thiamin, folic acid and potassium.

Ingredients   **4 portions**
300 ml skimmed milk   1 orange
1 dessertspoon acacia honey   10 gm cucumber peel
2 eggs

Nutritional analysis per portion
Energy: 88 KCals
Fibre: 1 g
Fat: 3.1 g

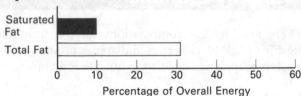

Percentage of Overall Energy

Method
1. Preheat the oven to 180°C, gas mark 4.
2. Wash the orange and peel off the zest. Reserve a little julienne of zest for garnish, and blanch the remainder in boiling water for one minute. Drain and chop into very fine dice.
3. Heat the milk gently and stir in honey to taste. Whisk the eggs and whisk in the sweetened milk. Add the orange zest. Ladle into little ramekins, cover individually with foil, and bake in a bain-marie.
4. Meanwhile, cut away the pith from the orange. Cut out the segments and squeeze out any remaining juice from the pulp. Reserve the segments and juice in the fridge.
5. When the custards are set, but not hard, remove from the oven. Chill and serve very cold, with the orange segments, a little juice and a garnish of julienne of orange peel and cucumber skin.

Carrotcake

Ingredients   10 portions

3 eggs (separated)   1 teaspoon bicarbonate of soda
15 ml sunflower oil   50 gm chopped walnuts
3 dessertspoons of clear honey   100 gm sultanas
250 gm wholemeal flour   250 gm carrots
1 teaspoon baking powder   cinnamon

Nutritional analysis per portion

Energy: 187 KCals
Fibre: 4 g
Fat: 6.4 g

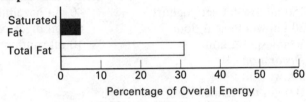

Percentage of Overall Energy

Method

1. Heat the oven to 180°C, gas mark 4. Grease and flour a tin, 18 cm (7″) in diameter.
2. Beat the egg yolk well with the honey. Stir in the fruit, nuts and grated carrot.
3. Sift together the dry ingredients, returning the bran to the bowl. Combine this with the fruit and nut mixture. If, depending on the size of the eggs, this mixture is too dry, add a little skimmed milk. Finally fold in the stiff egg whites. Fill the tin. Bake for about an hour or until a skewer comes out cleanly from the centre of the cake.
4. Turn out onto a cooling wire and cool. This cake can be served coated with a tangy, lemon-infused fromage frais.

Light 'n' Fruity Cheesecake

This is a version of Miriam Polunin's cheesecake, with the addition of ground, roasted hazelnuts in the cake base. The flavour of the roast nuts gently permeates the cheese topping during cooking.

Ingredients   **6 portions**

2 eggs (separated)   40 gm sultanas
250 gm quark or low-fat fromage   40 gm dried apricots
frais   1 teaspoonful zest of orange
150 ml low-fat set yoghurt   40 gm hazelnuts
30 gm wholemeal flour   60 gm digestive biscuits
1 tablespoon honey   10 ml sunflower oil
Decoration
3 kiwi fruit
100 gm red grapes

Nutritional analysis per portion
Energy: 238 KCals
Fibre: 4 g
Fat: 9 g

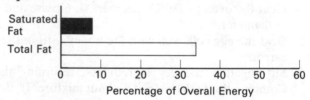

Percentage of Overall Energy

Method
1. Preheat the oven to 180°C, gas mark 4.
2. Roast the hazelnuts and remove most of the skins by rubbing them together between your hands. Reduce the biscuits to crumbs in the food processor. Add the nuts and reduce to very small nuggets.
3. Select a cake tin with releasable bottom, 18 cm (7") in diameter. Alternatively use a deep flan ring on a baking tray. Brush the sides and bottom with oil. Press down the crumb mixture as a base.
4. Chop up the apricots very finely. Soak in water and drain just before use.
5. Beat the egg yolks with the quark or fromage frais, flour and honey. Stir in the yoghurt, dried fruit and orange zest. Finally cut in the stiff egg whites. Pour into the tin and bake for 20–25 minutes, or until the edges are set but the centre is still soft and springy.
6. Allow to cool. The surface may crack on cooling but this is of no importance as it will be covered with alternate circles of half grapes and kiwi fruit slices for service. The nut and biscuit base is rather crumbly, as it has not been steeped with the usual melted butter. Consequently a little care and delicacy is required when slicing and serving.

Pineapple Sorbet

Ingredients
12 portions

2 large pineapples
2 large oranges

4 egg whites

Nutritional analysis per portion

Energy: 74 KCals
Fibre: 2 g
Fat: 0 g

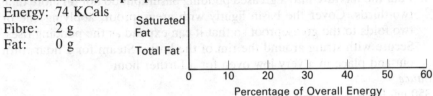

Method
1. Cut away the pineapples' outer layer. Remove the central hard core and cut the flesh into chunks.
2. On a fine grater, remove the orange zest. Blanch very briefly in boiling water. Add this and the orange juice to the pineapple pieces and liquidise.
3. Fold in the stiff egg whites. Pour into an ice cream machine, turn on and leave till firm – approximately half an hour. Scoop out into a container. This sorbet goes well with the 'Healthy crumble'.

Steamed Fruit Pudding with Light Yoghurt Sauce

Ingredients
10 portions

50 gm mixed nuts
80 gm raisins
200 gm stoned dates
1 egg
50 ml honey
50 ml sunflower oil

200 ml natural pineapple juice
300 gm wholemeal flour
$\frac{1}{4}$ teaspoon nutmeg
1 teaspoon cinnamon
1 level teaspoon bicarbonate soda
50 gm yoghurt

Nutritional analysis per portion

Energy: 299 KCals
Fibre: 5 g
Fat: 8.8 g

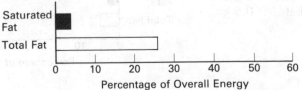

Method
1. Set the oven on low, at 120°C, gas mark $\frac{1}{2}$.
2. Chop the fruit and nuts together. Beat the egg, honey, oil and pineapple juice together. Stir in the fruit and nuts, and combine well.
3. Sift the flour, bicarbonate, nutmeg and cinnamon to achieve lightness, but do not discard the sifted bran/fibre. Add the flour to the fruit and nut mixture and stir in with the yoghurt.
4. Pour the mixture into a greased pudding basin, but do not fill more than two-thirds. Cover the basin lightly with greaseproof, applying one or two folds to the greaseproof so that it can expand as the pudding rises. Secure with string around the rim of the basin. Steam for 1 hour, turn out and place in a very low oven for a further hour.

Sauce
350 gm low-fat set yoghurt
2 dessertspoons of clear honey
3 egg whites

Method
1. Whisk the egg whites and, once they begin to fluff up, gradually dribble in the honey.
2. Continue whisking and, when the egg whites have increased gently in volume, but are not yet stiff, fold in the yoghurt.

Tangerine and Lemon Mousse

This is an airy citrus mousse which is an ideal dessert for Christmas time. Nectarines or satsumas can be used if tangerines are not available.

Ingredients   **5 portions**

225 gm low-fat natural yoghurt   150 ml orange juice (unsweetened)
100 gm low-fat curd cheese or   450 gm tangerines
quark   1 egg white
juice and rind of 1 large lemon   1 teaspoon of clear honey
25 gm powdered gelatine

Nutritional analysis per portion
Energy: 92 KCals
Fibre: 1 g
Fat: 0.5 g

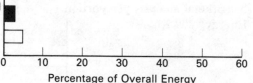

Method
1. Fill 5 moulds – dariole, crème caramel or ramekins – with water and stand in the fridge.
2. Cream together the yoghurt, cheese, honey, zest and juice of lemon, until there are no lumps.
3. Sprinkle the gelatine onto the cold orange juice and bring to the boil. Whisk in the gelatine. Allow to cool and fold one-third into the cheese and yoghurt mixture. Empty the moulds of water and half fill with this mixture. Place in a fridge or blast chiller to set.
4. While the orange juice is cooling, peel the tangerines, removing pith and pips. Liquidise the segments and press firmly through a strainer. Add the remaining two-thirds of the orange juice/setting agent to the tangerines, and fold in the stiff egg white. Spoon onto the set yoghurt mixture. Place in the fridge to chill over night.
5. For service, place the moulds briefly in hot water, and turn out.

Summer Fruit Tartlets

Use whichever seasonal fruit is in tiptop condition. Generally, the varieties that appear towards the end of summer are highest in fibre; just 100 gm of blackberries or blackcurrants contain 8 gm of fibre – a quarter of our recommended daily intake.

Ingredients   **6 portions**

Pastry   a little cold water
180 gm wholemeal flour   10 ml sunflower oil
90 gm polyunsaturated margarine

Crème Pâtissier   *Fruit and Coulis*
300 ml skimmed milk   250 gm strawberries
1 $\frac{1}{2}$ dessertspoons clear honey   250 gm blackcurrants
1 vanilla pod   1 dessertspoon of clear honey
2 egg yolks
20 gm wheatmeal flour
100 ml low-fat set yoghurt

Nutritional analysis per portion
Energy: 317 KCals
Fibre: 7 g
Fat: 16.8 g

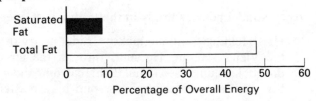

Method

Pastry

1. Set the oven to 180°C, gas mark 4.
2. Sift the flour and return the bran to the bowl. Incorporate the margarine by rubbing through your thumb and fingertips. Finally add some cold water so that all the ingredients can be kneaded into a ball; only a little water is required because the margarine is quite moist. Wrap in clingfilm and chill in the fridge for 40 minutes.
3. Carefully roll out the pastry as thinly as possible, lifting and turning regularly. The pastry must line 6 × 9 cm (3 $\frac{1}{2}''$) tartlet tins. If you do not have a large enough pastry cutter, cut out the shapes before the pastry is too thin, and roll out the circles individually.
4. Brush the tins with oil and line with pastry. Prick the bases with a fork and rest in he fridge for half an hour. Bake blind for approximately 12 minutes. Place on a cooling wire.

Crème Pâtissier

1. Gently bring the milk to a simmer, along with the honey and vanilla pod. Strain.
2. Combine the egg yolks and wheatmeal flour and gradually incorporate a quarter of the hot milk until you have a smooth consistency. Whisk this mixture into the remainder of the milk and return to a gentle heat, stirring constantly.
3. Once coating consistency has been reached, strain and leave to cool. Stir in the yoghurt.

Coulis

1. Gently cook the blackcurrants and honey with a drop of water, just to soften the fruit. Liquidise. If you strain the coulis it will have a more impressive sheen, but some of the fibre will be lost.
2. Coat the base of each plate with some coulis. Dribble lines of crème pâtissier upon the coulis and feather a pattern with a knife or skewer.
3. To serve, spoon some crème pâtissier into each pastry case. Slice the strawberries thinly and arrange decoratively. Place a tartlet upon each plate.

Healthy Apple Strudel

Apfel strudel belongs firmly in the tradition of Viennese cuisine.

Herr Heinrich Wittman makes strudel pastry daily in the patisserie of the Vienna Hilton. He spins through the air circles of transparent dough, kneading then in full flight, catching them on the knuckles of his fist – delicate porcelain plates spun by a master conjuror. He is not satisfied until they are as fine as tissue paper. His skill is such that it becomes a kind of performance art (Elizabeth Luard, *The Princess and the Peasant*, Bantam, p. 48).

We mortals might not be able to reproduce such a spectacle, but it should be within our capabilities to turn out a perfectly good strudel. As with the 'Salmon and lime strudel parcels' (p. 99), strong white flour is used, in the interests of achieving a wafer-thin pastry, the considerable fruit content of the recipe providing a fair amount of fibre.

Ingredients   **8 portions**

Filling   *Pastry*
1.2 kilos cooking apples   250 gm strong white flour
1 digestive biscuit (crushed)   1 egg and 1 egg yolk
100 gm sultanas   80 ml skimmed milk
a generous quantity of cinnamon   20 ml olive oil
powder $\frac{1}{2}$ egg (for egg wash)
30 gm polyunsaturated margarine
3–4 dessertspoons of clear honey

Nutritional analysis per portion
Energy: 289 KCals
Fibre: 5 g
Fat: 8.3 g

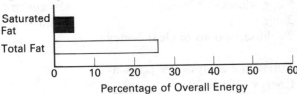

Method
1. Pre-heat the oven to 190°C, gas mark 5.
2. Incorporate the eggs into the flour and gradually add the milk and oil. Knead for several minutes, adding a little more flour if necessary, until you have a smooth dough. Leave to rest, covered, on a floured surface, for 30–40 minutes.
3. Peel, quarter and core the apples, and slice thinly. Mix together the apples, sultanas, biscuit crumbs, melted margarine, honey and cinnamon. Set aside in the fridge.
4. Roll out the pastry as thinly as possible, into a rectangle slightly longer than it is wide. Pick up the pastry and, with your fingertips or knuckles – whichever comes more easily – carefully pull the strudel out from the middle to the edges, until you can see your hands clearly through the pastry.
5. Trim the edges, and place the pastry on a lightly floured kitchen towel. Spread the fruit filling evenly on top, leaving an inch-wide gap at the borders. Fold the lengthwise borders on top of the fruit – this is to prevent the filling escaping while the strudel is being rolled up.

6. Pick up the ends of the towel and carefully roll up the strudel. Seal the final border with eggwash. Gently roll the strudel onto a lightly greased baking tray. Brush with eggwash and bake for 30–40 minutes.

Strawberry Carob Roll

Carob is a healthy alternative to chocolate, milled from the roast pulp of the carob bean. Applied too liberally, its flavour and deep dark colour will be overwhelming, so take care to use it in moderation. It contains none of the caffeine of cocoa powder, less than two-thirds the calories, and only 0.7% fat, compared with 23.7% in its conventional equivalent. It is high in natural sugar, thereby reducing the need for additional recipe sweetening.

Ingredients   **8 portions**

30 gm carob powder   250 gm low-fat set yoghurt
5 egg whites   450 gm strawberries
3 egg yolks   10 ml sunflower oil
2 $\frac{1}{2}$ dessertspoons of clear honey

Nutritional analysis per portion
Energy: 104 KCals
Fibre: 2 g
Fat: 3.7 g

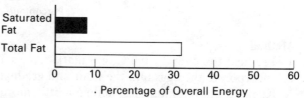

. Percentage of Overall Energy

Method

1. Set the oven to 180°C, gas mark 4. Lightly oil a Swiss roll tin and line with a lightly oiled sheet of greaseproof.
2. Beat together the egg yolks, honey and virtually all the sifted carob powder.
3. Whisk the egg whites till stiff and incorporate a quarter into the carob mixture. Carefully fold this in with the remaining whites. Pour evenly into the Swiss roll tin and bake until set but springy – approximately 12–15 minutes. Allow to rest for a couple of minutes.
4. Lightly dust a greaseproof with the remaining carob powder and turn the sponge onto it. Carefully remove the layer of the original grease-proof, and replace with a fresh sheet. Roll up the sponge as you would a Swiss roll and leave to cool.

5. Meanwhile, slice the strawberries thinly. When the roll is cool, unravel, smooth the yoghurt over with a palette-knife and cover with strawberries. Roll up again and allow to 'set' in the fridge. Serve in slices.

Summer Pudding

Use a combination of whichever berries are seasonably available. The tayberry is a relatively new product from Scotland, rather like an elongated dark raspberry. Strawberries are not just symbolic of English gardens and Wimbledon; they also provide a good amount of vitamin C.

Freshness is of the essence with all such perishable fruit. One summer I attempted this recipe using loganberries, raspberries and strawberries bought from a little farm at Kimmeridge on the Dorset coast. The flavour almost exploded on the tastebuds!

Ingredients   **6 portions**
750 gm summer berries –
strawberries, raspberries,
blackcurrants, blackberries,   a selection of 3 or 4 fruits
loganberries, tayberries
3 dessertspoons clear honey
8 slices of wholewheat bread,
crusts removed

Nutritional analysis per portion
Energy: 170 KCals
Fibre: 11 g
Fat: 1.3 g

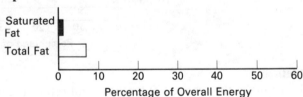

Method
1. Cook the berries gently under cover with the honey, for 5–10 minutes. Allow to cool and strain the fruit, reserving the juice.
2. Cut 2 circles (or 4 semi-circles) of bread to fit the top and bottom of a $1\frac{1}{2}$ pint pudding basin. Shape the remaining bread into oblongs (like thick 'soldiers') to fit round the sides.
3. Dip the bread in the fruit juice and line the basin. Fill with fruit, cover with the top 'lid' of bread, and spoon over some more juice, so that all the bread is well soaked.

4. Place a saucer on top, apply a weight and leave in the fridge overnight.
5. Turn out and serve.

Pear Souffle´ Pancakes

Pancakes offer the opportunity to wrap up various fillings within light, tempting litle parcels. It could be an apple, sultana and cinnamon mixture drawn from an autumn windfall, or the soft cheese filling of 'blintzes' . . . the range is almost limitless. In this recipe, ripe, juicy pears are used to make soufflé pancakes.

Ingredients   **10 portions**
Batter   *Filling*
120 gm wheatmeal flour   800 gm ripe pears
1 large egg $\frac{1}{2}$ lemon
300 ml skimmed milk   2–3 dessertspoons honey
                                      30 ml cognac
                                      4 egg yolks
                                      5 egg whites
                                      1 vanilla pod
                                      15 gm polyunsaturated margarine

Nutritional analysis per portion
Energy: 139 KCals
Fibre: 3 g
Fat: 4.6 g

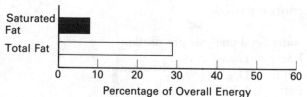

Percentage of Overall Energy

Method
1. To make the crêpes, sift the flour and return the bran to the bowl. Beat in the egg and gradually incorporate the milk until a smooth batter is obtained. Rest in the fridge for an hour.
2. Heat the crêpe pan; if it has been well proved there will be no need to use any fat as a frying medium. Swill a little batter round the pan, to a wafer-thin consistency. Return to a high heat for about 30 seconds, toss over and lightly brown the other side.
3. Set the oven to 210°C, gas mark 7. Grease a baking sheet with the melted margarine.
4. Peel, quarter and core the pears. Cook out gently under cover with the cognac, lemon juice, honey and split vanilla pod.

5. When the fruit has cooked and softened, remove the pod and blend the mixture in the food processor with the egg yolks.
6. Whisk the egg whites to soft peaks and cut into the pear mixture. Place a large spoonful in the middle of a pancake and gently fold over. Space the pancakes out well on the baking sheet. They will rise in a hot oven after about 10 minutes. Serve immediately.
7. This dish can be served with apricot or raspberry sauce. Indeed, a little of the raspberry and orange soup (p. 76) would double as a perfect coulis!

Banana Bread

Ingredients
10 good portions

4 very ripe bananas
60 ml skimmed milk
1 vanilla pod
2 eggs
20 gm polyunsaturated margarine
2 dessertspoons clear honey

225 gm wholemeal flour
1 ½ teaspoons bicarbonate of soda
½ teaspoon nutmeg
1 ½ teaspoons mixed spice
10 ml sunflower oil

Nutritional analysis per portion
Energy: 155 KCals
Fibre: 3 g
Fat: 4.5 g

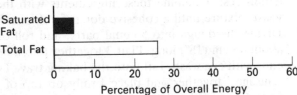

Method
1. Preheat the oven to 180°C, gas mark 4.
2. Place the vanilla pod and milk in a small pan and warm gently, so that the vanilla flavour infuses into the milk. Remove the pod. Add the margarine and allow it to melt.
3. Blend the bananas in a food processor, and add the eggs, milk and honey. Blend again. Alternatively, for a chunkier texture, merely mash the bananas and combine with the other ingredients; or perhaps add a finely diced stick of dried banana.
4. Sift the flour, spices and bicarbonate into a bowl. Return the bran/fibre to the bowl. Incorporate the banana mixture thoroughly, and pour into a lightly oiled loaf tin (2 lb size). Bake for 45 minutes, or until a knife comes cleanly out of the centre.
5. Turn out onto a cooling wire.

Plaited Fruit Loaf

Ingredients   10 good portions

50 ml sunflower oil   zest of lemon
150 ml skimmed milk   100 gm raisins
2 dessertspoons clear honey   25 gm mixed nuts
25 gm fresh yeast   80 gm dried apricots
1 egg   450 gm wholemeal flour

Nutritional analysis per portion

Energy: 259 KCals
Fibre: 7 g
Fat: 7.7 g

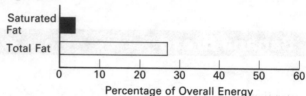

Percentage of Overall Energy

Method

1. Preheat the oven to 180°C, gas mark 4.
2. Lightly oil a baking tray. Sift the flour, returning the bran to the bowl. Warm the flour above a range or in a low oven with the door open.
3. Warm the milk and stir in the oil and honey. When cooled to lukewarm, whisk in the yeast and set aside for 5 minutes in a warm place.
4. Chop the nuts, apricot and raisins and mix together with the grated lemon zest. Combine these ingredients with the flour and stir in the yeast mixture until a cohesive dough is obtained.
5. Divide the dough into 5 equal parts, and roll out into sausage shapes about 45 cm (18″) long. Plait 3 together into a braid and seal down the ends with egg wash. Lift onto the baking tray. Twist the remaining two 'sausages' together and place firmly on top of the braid, sealing the ends. Cover with a damp cloth and leave to prove in a warm location for an hour.
6. Brush with egg wash and bake in the oven for 45 minutes.

Granary, Oat and Walnut Loaf

It is appropriate that this section should end with a bread recipe, as, in its unadulterated form, bread comprises a staple component of any healthy diet. This recipe is particularly nutritious, with walnuts contributing the essential linoleic acid, and oats rich in 'gummy' fibre. The special flavour of this loaf places a new interpretation upon James Oppenheim's verse:

> Give us bread
> but give us roses.

Ingredients   10 portions

350 gm malted brown flour	1 teaspoon honey
80 gm oats	5 gm salt
80 gm walnuts	15 gm fresh yeast
300 ml skimmed milk	$\frac{1}{2}$ egg
10 ml olive oil	

Nutritional analysis per portion
Energy: 213 KCals
Fibre: 3 g
Fat: 6.8 g

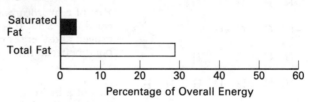

Method
1. Sift the flour and return the bran to the bowl. Add the oats, finely chopped walnuts and salt. Mix together and place the bowl in a very low oven for 5 minutes, with the door ajar.
2. Warm the milk to blood heat and stir in the honey. Pour a little of the milk over the yeast and allow to stand for a few minutes. Stir the yeast to a smooth paste.
3. Add the yeast ferment and all the milk to the dry ingredients, combining well until the mixture comes away from the sides of the bowl.
4. Cover and leave to prove for $1\frac{1}{2}$ hours.
5. Set the oven to 220°C, gas mark 7, and brush a 2 lb loaf tin with oil.
6. Knock back the dough and knead for 3–4 minutes. Lay inside the loaf tin and leave to prove for a further 40 minutes.
7. Brush with egg wash and bake for 15 minutes at 220°C (mark 7) and 15 minutes at 200°C (mark 6). Turn out of the tin and return to the oven for a further 10 minutes at 180°C (mark 4).

Appendix I Diagrammatic Representation of Types of Fatty Acids

```
 H   H   H   H
 |   |   |   |
-C - C - C - C -
 |   |   |   |
 H   H   H   H
```

Part of a hydrocarbon chain of **saturated** fatty acid. The carbon chain is saturated with hydrogen.

```
 H   H   H   H   H
 |   |   |   |   |
-C - C - C = C - C -
 |   |           |
 H   H           H
```

Part of a hydrocarbon chain of **monounsaturated** fatty acid. It is not saturated with hydrogen and there is one (mono) double bond between the carbon atoms.

```
 H   H   H   H   H   H   H
 |   |   |   |   |   |   |
-C - C = C - C - C = C - C -
 |       |           |
 H       H           H
```

Part of a hydrocarbon chain of **polyunsaturated** fatty acid. It is not saturated with hydrogen and there are several (poly) double bonds between the carbon atoms.

138

Appendix II Conversion of Fat by Weight into Kilocalories

The Example of Rabbit

Energy, in calories per 100 gm	Amount of fat, grams	Amount of energyderived from fat	Proportion of energy derived from fat
124	4.0	36	29%

1 gram of fat contains 9 kilocalories, so the 4 gm of fat in a 100 gm portion of rabbit contains 36 kilocalories. NACNE and COMA express their dietary fat recommendations as the percentage of overall energy derived from fat. To work this out, simply divide the amount of energy derived from fat by the total amount of energy the food item provides:

$$\frac{36}{124} = 0.29$$

Which expressed as a percentage, is 29 per cent.

Exactly the same procedure can be carried ot with other nutrients:

Protein   contains   4.0   kilocalories per gram
Carbohydrate contains   3.75 kilocalories per gram
Alcohol   contains   7.0   kilocalories per gram

So, staying with rabbit, 100 gm contains 22 gm of protein, which equals 88 kilocalories:

$$\frac{88}{124} = 0.71 \times \frac{100}{1} = 71\%$$

Hence rabbit derives 71 per cent of its energy from protein and 29 per cent from fat.

Appendix III The Meaning Behind the 'E' Numbers

Colourings

Beware	Suspect	Safe
Azo Dyes		
E100		E100 Turmeric
E101		E101 Vitamin B2
E102 Tartrazine		E102
E104 Quinoline Yellow		E104
107 Yellow 2G		107
E110 Sunset Yellow		E110
E120 Cochineal		E120
E122 Carmoisine, Azorubine		E122
E123 Amaranth		E123
E124 Ponceau 4R		E124
E127 Erythrosine		E127
128 Red 2G		128
E131 Patent Blue V		E131
E132 Indigo Carmine		E132
133 Brilliant Blue		133
		E140 Chlorophyll
		E141
E142 Green S		E142
	Lissamine Green	
E150	E150 Caramel	
E151 Black PN		E151
E153		E153 Carbon
154 Brown FK		154
155 Brown HT		155
E160		E160 Relatives of
E161		E161 Vitamin F
E162		

E163 Anthocyanins
E170 Chalk
E171 Titanium Oxide
E172 Iron Oxides

E173 Aluminium
E174 Silver
E175 Gold

E180 Pigment Rubine

Preservatives

Safe

E200 ⎫
E201 ⎬ Sorbates
E202 ⎪
E203 ⎭

Suspect

Beware

E210 ⎫
E211 ⎬ Benzoates
E212 ⎪
E213 ⎭

E214 ⎫
E215 ⎪
E216 ⎬ Complex benzoates
E217 ⎪
E218 ⎪
E219 ⎭

E220 ⎫
E221 ⎪
E222 ⎪
E223 ⎬ Sulphites, Sulphur Dioxide
E224 ⎪
E226 ⎭

E-number	Beware	Suspect	Safe
E227	Sulphites		
E230	} Biphenyls		
E231	} Biphenyls		
E232	} Biphenyls		
E233			} On citrus and banana skins
E234			} On citrus and banana skins
E236		} Formates	
E237		} Formates	
E238		} Formates	
E239	Hexamine		
E249	} Nitrites		
E250	} Nitrites		
E251	} Nitrites		
E252	Nitrate		
E260			} Acetates (Vinegar)
E261			} Acetates (Vinegar)
E262			} Acetates (Vinegar)
E263			} Acetates (Vinegar)
E270		Lactic Acid	
E280			} Propionates
E281			} Propionates
E282			} Propionates
E283			} Propionates
E290		Carbon Dioxide	
E296			E296
E297			E297

Anti-oxidants, Emulsifiers, Stabilisers, Miscellaneous

Safe

E300, E301, E302, E304 } Ascorbates

E306, E307, E308, E309 } Vitamin E

E322 Lecithins

E330, E331, E332, E333 } Citrates

E334, E335, E336, E337 } Tartrates

E338, E339, E340 } Phosphates

Suspect

E325, E326, E327 } Lactates

Beware

E310, E311, E312 } Gallates

E320 BHA

E321 BHT

E300
E301
E302
E304
E306
E307
E308
E309
E310
E311
E312
E320
E321
E322
E325
E326
E327
E330
E331
E332
E333
E334
E335
E336
E337
E338
E339
E340

Safe

E341	Phosphates
350	
351	} Malates
352	
353	Metatartaric Acid
355	Adipic Acid
363	Succinic Acid
375	Vitamin B
380	} Citrates
381	
E385	
E400	
E401	
E402	
E403	} Alginates (seaweed)
E404	
E405	
E406	Agar
E410	}
E412	} Natural Gums
E413	}
E415	} Natural Gums
E416	}
E420	Sorbitol
E421	
E422	Glycerol

Suspect

370	Heptonolactone
E385	Salt of EDTA
E407	Carrageenan
E414	Acacia Gum
E421	Mannitol
432	} Polyoxyethylenes
433	

Beware

430	} Stearates
431	

434		434		434
435		435 Polyoxyethylenes		435
436		436		436
E440			E440 Pectin	E440
442		442 Ammonium phosphatides		442
E450	E450 Polyphosphates			E450
E460			E460	E460
E461			E461	E461
E463			E463 Celluloses	E463
E464			E464	E464
E465			E465	E465
E466			E466	E466
E470		E470		E470
E471		E471		E471
E472		E472 Fats, soaps		E472
E473		E473		E473
E474		E474		E474
E475		E475		E475
E476		E476 Fats, soaps		E476
E477		E477		E477
E478		E478		E478
E481		E481		E481
E482		E482 Fatty acids		E482
E483		E483		E483
491		491		491
492		492		492
493		493 Sorbitans		493
494		494		494
495		495		495
500			500	500
501			501	501
502			502 Carbonates	502
503			503	503
504			504	504
507		507 Chlorides		

Number	Beware	Suspect	Safe
508		Chlorides	
509		(Chlorides)	
510		(Chlorides)	
513		Sulphuric Acid	
514		Sodium Sulphate	
515			Potassium Sulphate
516			Calcium Sulphate
518			Magnesium Sulphate
524		Caustic Soda	
525		Caustic Potash	
526			Calcium Hydroxide
527		Ammonium Hydroxide	
528			Magnesium Hydroxide
529		Quick Lime	
530		Magnesium Oxide	
535	Ferrocyanides		
536	(Ferrocyanides)		
541	Phosphate		
542		Bone Phosphate	
544	Polyphosphates		
545	(Polyphosphates)		
551			Silicates
552			(Silicates)
553			Talc
554	Silicates		
556	(Silicates)		
558		Bentonite	
559			Kaolin
570			Stearate
572			(Stearate)
575		Glucono delta Lactone	

576		576 Gluconates	576
577		577 Gluconates	577
578		578 Gluconates	578

Flavour Enhancers

620	620 Glutamic Acid		620
621	621 Monosodium Glutamate		621
622	622 Other Glutamates		622
623	623 Other Glutamates		623
627	627 Guanylate		627
631	631 Inosinate		631
635	635 Guanylate and Inosinate		635
636	636 Maltol 'fresh bake' flavour		636
637	637 Ethyl Maltol – sweetener		637
900	900 Dimethicone		900
901		901 Bees Wax	901
903		903 Carnauba Wax	903
904		904 Shellac	904
905	905 Mineral Hydrocarbons		905
907		907 Wax	907
920		920 Amino-acid derivative	920
924	924 Bromate		924
925	925 Chlorine		925
927	927 Azoformamide		927

148

Notes to Appendix III:

Acacia gum   Known to be toxic at 100%; some confections get to 45%.
Acids and alkalis   These are all corrosive in sufficient quantity. Little information is available as to how they are used.
Aluminium   Suspected to be capable of harm in some people.
Azo dyes   Dangerous to asthmatics, hyperactive children, those sensitive to aspirin.
Benzoates   Dangerous to allergics, asthmatics, hypersensitives.
BHA/BHT   Currently subjects of intensive safety research, because of many doubts. Either may contribute indirectly to wastage of body stores of vitamin D, or cause hyperactivity. Neither permitted in foods intended for young children.
Biphenyls   Beware on citrus fruit. Some probably penetrates to the flesh.
Bleaches   Doubts exist about safety. In flour destroys vitamin E and other variants. Capable of major intestinal upset and convulsions.
Bone phosphate   Vegetarians would wish to avoid this.
Caramel   Prepared by various processes, some of which may incur vitamin B_6 deficiency. 98% by weight of all the colouring used in food.
Carrageenan   Irish moss, a seaweed; may cause ulcerative colitis, and may decompose to a carcinogen. Used mostly in drinks.
Chlorides   Several are capable of corrosive effects on the intestine and perhaps disturbances of body fluids. Very little information available.
Cochineal   Can cause hyperactivity in children.
EDTA   May disrupt absorption of iron, zinc and copper.
Ferrocyanides   We depend for our safety on nothing disturbing their low absorption from the intestine.
Flavour enhancers   Make the food taste better than it really is. Along with salt and sugar, largely responsible for distorting appetites and encouraging over-eating.
Formates   Formic acid very irritant to the skin. All have diuretic effects (on the kidneys).
Gallates   A benzoate not permitted in foods intended for young children. May harm asthmatics, those sensitive to aspirin, hyperactive children.
Hexamine   May upset intestines and urinary system. Possibly cancer forming.
Hydrocarbons   That is, liquid paraffins, which as cathartics may cause anal seepage and stool looseness in some people.
Lactic acid   Beware in food for very small babies.
Mannitol   Occasionally produces hypersensitivity.
Nitrate, nitrite   Highly controversial. May combine with amines in the stomach, producing highly cancer-forming nitrosamines. Interacts dangerously with the blood cells of infants.
Polyphosphates   Used to retain moisture in meat products, they can easily be abused to inflate the weight (and price) of a product.
Polyoxyethelenes   Very little information available; may alter the absorption of fat.
Propionates   Migraine sufferers may do well to avoid these.
Purines   Prohibited from foods intended for young children. Gout sufferers and rheumatics generally, should avoid these.
Sorbitan esters   Very little information available. May increase gut absorption of paraffins, which are an irritant.
Stearates   May produce skin allergies; a possible cause of kidney stones.
Sulphur dioxide   Beware on uncooked raw fruit. Dangerous to asthmatics and hypersensitives. Lowers vitamin E content of flour. Lowers vitamin B_1, content of various foods.

This material has been reproduced by kind permission of the Soil Association. Information about their work, particularly relating to organic standards, can be obtained from The Soil Association, 86 Colston Street, Bristol, BS1 5BB.

Appendix IV The Sources and Functions of Vitamins and Minerals

Table A1 Vitamins

Vitamin	Food sources	Utilised in
A Retinol or Carotene	Carrots, green leafy veg, eggs, dairy produce, liver	Colour and night vision; skin; connective tissue
B_1 Thiamin	Milk, meat, bread, cereals, potatoes, nuts	Carbohydrate metabolism; central nervous system (CNS)
B_2 Riboflavin	Milk, meat, eggs, vegetables	Fat and protein metabolism; vision; skin
Niacin	Meat, potatoes, bread, fish, peanuts	Carbohydrate and fat metabolism
B_5 Pantothenic acid	Meat, milk, cereals, pulses	Energy metabolism
B_6 Pyridoxin	Meat, fish, green leafy veg, potatoes, grains	Production of red blood cells; CNS
B_{12} Cyanocobalamin	Meat, fish, dairy produce	Production of red blood cells; CNS
Folic acid	Offal, green leafy veg, cereals	Production of red blood cells; CNS
C Ascorbic acid	Green leafy veg, fruit, potatoes	Iron absorption; healing and resistance to infection
D calciferols	Dairy produce, oily fish, eggs; also derived from sunshine	Bones, teeth and growth
E Tocopherols	Vegetable oils, green leafy veg, eggs	Protection of vitamins A & C and fatty acids, from oxidative damage
K	Green leafy veg, cauliflower, liver	Blood clotting; fat digestion

Table A2 Minerals

Mineral	Food sources	Utilised in
Sodium	Salt, bread, dairy products, meat products	Maintenance of constant body water content
Potassium	Vegetables, fruit, meat, milk, nuts	Maintenance of constant body water content
Chlorine	Salt, bread, dairy products, meat products	Assisting sodium and potassium
Calcium	Dairy products, green veg., sardines, nuts	Bones and teeth; blood clotting
Magnesium	Dairy produce, green veg., potatoes	Bone formation; energy metabolism
Phosphorous	Milk, cereals, meat	Bones and teeth; energy metabolism
Iron	Meat, nuts, seeds, green veg., potatoes	Red blood cell formation
Zinc	Meat, milk, seafood, green veg.	Growth and bones; immune system; taste; insulin release
Copper	Meat, nuts, grains, vegetables, shellfish	Growth; enzyme synthesis
Fluoride	Seafood, water, tea	Tooth structure
Iodine	Dairy produce, eggs, seafood	Thyroid function
Manganese	Cereals, nuts, tea, dried fruit	Enzyme synthesis
Chromium	Meat, dairy produce, cereals, vegetables	Enhancement of the action of insulin
Selenium	Cereals, meat, fish, dairy produce	Protection of membranes from oxidative damage

Recipe Index